Fleet Air Arm

British Carrier Aviation, 1939-1945

By Ron Mackay

Color by Don Greer

squadron/signal publications

Two Supermarine Seafires of A Flight, 808 Squadron aboard the escort carrier HMS BATTLER shot down a Focke-Wulf Fw 200 Condor over the Bay of Biscay on 24 June 1943. The Condor was shadowing a convoy traveling from Gibraltar to Britain. Lt P. Constable, the Flight Commander, flew a Seafire L Mk IIC (A/NM970), while Sub-Lt A.G. Penney piloted a Seafire Mk IIC (F/MB302).

Acknowledgements

Imperial War Museum (IWM), London
Bruce Robertson
Harry Holmes
Ray Sturtivant
Bill Penlington
Dick Ward
J.D.R. Rawlings
US Army

Dedication:

This book is dedicated to the men of the Fleet Air Arm who, whether serving as aircrew or support personnel, fought against mighty odds for the first three years of World War Two. Their courage, fortitude and endurance witnessed the ultimate creation of a first-rate Naval Air Force during the second half of that global conflict.

Specific thanks goes to the small band of naval airmen of the Air Crew Association (Northwest Essex Branch) and in particular to Malcolm Brown (Seafire pilot) and Bill Penlington (Swordfish pilot). Their support over the years in bringing this project to fruition is truly appreciated.

ISBN 0-89747-432-5

If you have any photographs of aircraft, armor, soldiers or ships of any nation, particularly wartime snapshots, why not share them with us and help make Squadron/Signal's books all the more interesting and complete in the future. Any photograph sent to us will be copied and the original returned. The donor will be fully credited for any photos used. Please send them to:

Squadron/Signal Publications, Inc.
1115 Crowley Drive
Carrollton, TX 75011-5010

Если у вас есть фотографии самолетов, вооружения, солдат или кораблей любой страны, особенно, снимки времен войны, поделитесь с нами и помогите сделать новые книги издательства Эскадрон/Сигнал еще интереснее. Мы переснимем ваши фотографии и вернем оригиналы. Имена приславших снимки будут сопровождать все опубликованные фотографии. Пожалуйста, присылайте фотографии по адресу:

Squadron/Signal Publications, Inc.
1115 Crowley Drive
Carrollton, TX 75011-5010

軍用機、装甲車両、兵士、軍艦などの写真を所持しておられる方は いらっしゃいませんか？どの国のものでも結構です。作戦中に撮影されたものが特に良いのです。Squadron/Signal社の出版する刊行物において、このような写真は内容を一層充実し、興味深くすることができます。当方にお送り頂いた写真は、複写の後お返しいたします。出版物中に写真を使用した場合は、必ず提供者のお名前を明記させて頂きます。お写真は下記にご送付ください。

Squadron/Signal Publications, Inc.
1115 Crowley Drive
Carrollton, TX 75011-5010

(Previous Page) A Supermarine Seafire fighter – believed to be a Seafire Mk IB – assigned to No 842 Squadron (Sqdn) is safely recovered aboard the escort carrier HMS (His Majesty's Ship) FENCER. Crewmen ran from the flight deck's edge toward the aircraft, whose arrestor hook had grabbed one of the arrestor cables. Two other cables are placed forward of the Seafire. The FENCER was built in the United States as USS CROATAN (AVG-14) before being transferred to the Royal Navy in 1943. No 842 Sqdn received its first Seafires in July of 1943, shortly before embarking on the FENCER. The carrier served in the Atlantic and Pacific oceans before being returned to the US at the end of 1946. (W. Penlington Collection)

Introduction

The Fleet Air Arm (FAA) of Britain's Royal Navy (RN) was a force suffering more than its share of problems between the two World Wars. Only from 1942 onwards did the Admiralty's 'Battleship Brigade' supporters concede the supremacy of aircraft over warships. Prior to that, the aircraft was basically regarded as an observation platform for naval gunnery, or for reconnaissance to seek out an adversary's Fleet.

Defense of the British Fleet from aerial or submarine attack was accorded low priority. The range of aircraft types on hand as World War Two approached generally ranged in quality of performance from indifferent to downright lethal. Additionally, control of the FAA was vested in the Royal Air Force (RAF) until 1937. The loss of numerous RAF skilled craftsmen when control was handed over to the Admiralty left a dangerous technical vacuum, but FAA personnel made their best efforts to retain technical proficiency during this period.

The FAA proved the worth of air-launched torpedoes in such episodes as the crippling of the Italian Fleet at Taranto in 1940 and the **BISMARCK** action. (These attacks had unfortunate consequences for other nations in World War Two). The protection of convoys helped to ensure that the Atlantic Lifeline remained intact. Aircraft designed for carrier operations – including Grumman and Chance-Vought designs from the United States – entered FAA service as the conflict progressed. These new machines enabled a steadily expanding FAA to go on the offensive in theatres ranging from the Arctic and Atlantic across to the Indian and Pacific Oceans. By 1945, British and Commonwealth naval aviators had truly demonstrated their worth in ensuring the successful outcome of World War Two.

Early Days

The Naval Wing of the Royal Flying Corps (RFC) was created in 1912. One year later, the cruiser **HMS HERMES** was fitted with a deck for launching amphibian aircraft. The RFC's Naval Wing was renamed the Royal Naval Air Service (RNAS) on 1 July 1914 – just over one month before Britain entered World War One. In that conflict's first three years, RNAS activities primarily involved seaplanes and fighters. The latter were used to attack German Zeppelins (dirigibles) 'shadowing' the Home Fleet. British airships performed anti-submarine patrols. No 8 (Naval) Squadron, an RNAS fighter unit under RFC control, operated on the Western Front in Europe.

On 26 June 1917, the battlecruiser **HMS FURIOUS** was commissioned. She was equipped with a flying deck forward of the superstructure, while retaining a single 18 inch (45.7 CM) gun on the aft deck. Squadron Commander E.H. Dunning successfully landed his Sopwith Pup fighter on the FURIOUS on 2 August 1917. The flight deck lacked arresting cables; instead, deck crewmen grabbed special rope toggles fitted to Dunning's Pup. The 3-knot (3.5 MPH/5.6 KMH) speed margin between ship and aircraft made it easy for the deck crew to grab the Pup. Five days later, Dunning made a second landing attempt aboard the FURIOUS; however, his Pup overshot the flight deck. The aircraft stalled before crashing into the sea and Dunning was drowned.

On 1 April 1918, the RNAS and the RFC were merged to form the Royal Air Force (RAF) – the world's first independent air arm. The RAF's formation resulted in the Air Ministry taking charge of naval aviation from the Admiralty. The Fleet Air Arm (FAA) was formed as a branch of the RAF in 1924 and would not come under RN control until 1937.

In 1918, the former Italian liner **CONTE ROSSO** was fitted with a long flush deck and named **HMS ARGUS**. HMS HERMES (II) – the first purpose-designed carrier built – entered service in 1924, followed by **HMS EAGLE** later that year. The latter vessel featured a bridge structure on the center starboard side, which became standard on all subsequent RN carriers. In 1925, HMS FURIOUS returned to service after an extensive refit to complete the RN's carrier strength for most of the 1920s. Joining these ships in service were the converted battlecruisers **HMS COURAGEOUS** in 1928 and **HMS GLORIOUS** two years later.

Great Britain entered the 1930s with more aircraft carriers (six) than either the United States (three) or Japan (three). The British ships were inferior to their US and Japanese counterparts in both aircraft carrying capacity and maximum speed (approximately three knots less). The FAA's modest strength of 130 aircraft – all biplanes – meant that there were more than sufficient vessels to accommodate this overall number of aircraft.

The first modern British carrier was the **HMS ARK ROYAL**, launched in 1937 – the same year the FAA won full operational independence from the RAF. By this stage of development, carriers were equipped with lateral arrester wires and flexible screens to prevent aircraft from toppling overboard. A flexible barrier designed to prevent aircraft missing the arrester wires from crashing into any parked aircraft was also fitted. Additionally, the ARK ROYAL had armor protection for her fuel and ammunition compartments.

The **ILLUSTRIOUS** class carriers introduced in 1940 had armor protection extended to their flight decks, but the ILLUSTRIOUS, the **FORMIDABLE**, and the **VICTORIOUS** featured only two lifts (US=eleva-

The Blackburn Dart torpedo-bomber entered FAA service in 1923. Approximately 70 examples served worldwide until 1935. The Dart's solid landing gear – split to allow for torpedo or bomb carriage – was a prized asset for a carrier-based aircraft. FAA aircraft wore Aluminum dope finish on their fabric-covered surfaces, while metal surfaces were left unpainted.

The Blackburn Blackburn entered service as a spotter/reconnaissance aircraft in 1923. The high cockpit position gave the pilot good forward visibility for takeoffs and landings. Spotters looked out from within the fuselage through two portholes on each fuselage side. The Blackburn was removed from the FAA inventory in 1931, four years ahead of the Dart.

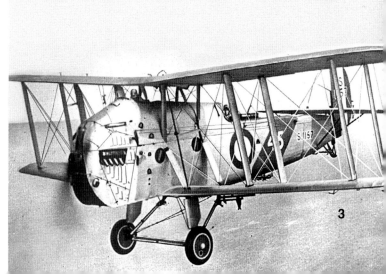

HMS FURIOUS was originally designed as a battlecruiser with two 18-inch (45.7 CM) main guns. A flight deck replaced the forward turret when she was commissioned on 67 June 1917, while the aft main gun was retained. A fatal accident during deck landing trials in 1917 resulted in the landing deck being placed aft of the superstructure, with ramps flanking the superstructure to maneuver aircraft forward. The FURIOUS retained this configuration until she was rebuilt with a flush flight deck in 1925.

tors) compared to the ARK ROYAL's three. Equally important for survival prospects was the provision of flash-proof compartments around the hangars and extractor fans for drawing off gasoline fumes. Asbestos or steel fire-curtains were placed in the hangars of the ILLUSTRIOUS class **INDOMITABLE** and the later fleet carriers **INDEFATIGABLE** and **IMPLACABLE**. The latter three ships also had extended internal hangar space. Finally, the lifts on the latter two vessels could accommodate aircraft weighing nine tons (8.2 MT), compared to the other four carriers' limitation of six tons (5.4 MT).

The FAA had only 220 aircraft when World War Two began on 1 September 1939. The only monoplane type in FAA service was the Blackburn **Skua**, a fighter/dive-bomber with moderate speed and bomb-carrying capability. The other aircraft types were biplanes, including the Fairey **Swordfish** torpedo-bomber, the Gloster **Sea Gladiator** fighter, and the Supermarine **Walrus** and Fairey **Seafox** spotter aircraft. The RN seemed to court disaster by pitting this motley collection against a modern Luftwaffe and the heavy anti-aircraft (AA) armament of German warships.

FAA aircraft prior to World War Two were finished in overall Aluminum Dope (FS17178) on fabric-covered surfaces. Metal surfaces were originally left unpainted, but later painted Cerrux Grey (FS16440) for protection against corrosion.

A Blackburn Ripon releases its torpedo into the water during an exercise in February of 1932. The aircraft was assigned to D Flight at Gosport, England, home to the Royal Navy's Torpedo School. The Ripon entered service in 1929, superceding the Dart as the FAA's principal torpedo-bomber. Blackburn built 92 Ripons, which served until 1935.

Two 'vee' formations of No 810 Squadron Blackburn Baffins take off from Gosport, near the Portsmouth Naval Base. The Baffin replaced the Ripon in FAA service from January of 1935, although the newer aircraft's overall performance was only marginally better than the Ripon. The Fairey Swordfish replaced the Baffin in the torpedo-bomber role in 1937.

Pre-War Carrier Identification Band Colors	
Ship	**Color (Approximate FS Color)**
ARGUS	Green (FS14187)
FURIOUS	Red (FS11136)
HERMES	White (FS17778)
EAGLE	Black (FS17078)
COURAGEOUS	Blue (FS15056)
GLORIOUS	Yellow (FS13538)
ARK ROYAL	Blue/Red/Blue

Individual Aircraft Fleet Numbers, 1924-39

Flight (Squadron) No	Code Range
401 Onwards	1-19
420 Onwards	20-39
440 Onwards	40-59
460 Onwards	60-89

Fleet Numbers were displayed on the fuselage band in Black or White, depending upon the band's color.

HMS HERMES was the first British aircraft carrier designed for this role and was commissioned in July of 1923. She had a low deck profile compared to other Royal Navy carriers. The aft flight deck was raised in a shallow curve and supported by twin pillar structures. The HERMES was built with her superstructure on the starboard side of her flight deck, which was similar to the superstructure fitted to her near contemporary, HMS EAGLE. HMS HERMES was sunk by Japanese carrier aircraft off Ceylon (now Sri Lanka) on 9 April 1942.

During the inter-war period, several FAA aircraft designs were adopted to carry floats instead of landing gear. One example was the Hawker Osprey fighter-reconnaissance aircraft, a derivative of the Royal Air Force's Hart light bomber. The Osprey entered service with FAA carrier-based squadrons and catapult flights in 1932 and was only declared obsolete in 1940.

This float-equipped Flycatcher flies above Mediterranean Fleet warships moored at Gibraltar during the early 1930s. The carrier HMS ARGUS was anchored near three battlecruisers (L-R): RENOWN, REPULSE, and HOOD. The latter two warships were sunk in 1941, the REPULSE by Japanese aircraft and the HOOD by the German battleship BISMARCK.

The Fairey Flycatcher was the first purpose-built British carrier fighter and served in this role from 1924 until 1934. Previous FAA fighters were adaptations of existing Royal Air Force (RAF) fighter aircraft. This Flycatcher operated from RAF Leuchars, Scotland, which served as a holding base for carrier-based aircraft assigned to the Home Fleet.

This No 810 Squadron Blackburn Shark (645/K4362) was finished in overall Aluminum dope and natural metal with black on the upper fuselage. The blue fuselage band was assigned to aircraft from HMS COURAGEOUS. The Shark torpedo-bomber had a long arrestor hook mounted under the aft fuselage.

No 820 Sqdn Sharks prepare to launch from the COURAGEOUS during the mid-1930s, while Baffins are spotted aft of the Sharks. The COURAGEOUS and her sister ship the GLORIOUS could each handle up to 48 aircraft. Both FAA and RAF personnel served as deck handlers on Royal Navy carriers until the FAA came under Royal Navy control in 1937.

Three Hawker Nimrod Mk Is of No 800 Sqdn fly over their ship, HMS COURAGEOUS. The aircraft had blue fuselage bands, while the lead aircraft's colored vertical stabilizer indicated either a flight or squadron commander's aircraft.

Fairey Swordfish Mk Is of No 823 Sqdn from HMS GLORIOUS pass the Royal Yacht VICTORIA AND ALBERT and a NELSON class battleship during the Naval Review at Spithead, England. This 1937 review celebrated the coronation of King George VI. The Swordfish had yellow fuselage bands to indicate assignment to the GLORIOUS. Black and white stripes on K5972's tail indicated a Squadron Leader.

Deck handlers complete folding the wings of a Swordfish Mk I (684/L2731) of No 821 Sqdn aboard the ARK ROYAL. The three-digit code on the fuselage and upper wing undersurface was replaced with letter/number codes in May of 1939. Deck handlers wore lightweight footwear for ease of movement on the flight deck.

Swordfish Mk Is assigned to No 810 Sqdn fly in formation in late 1937. The blue fuselage bands for the COURAGEOUS' aircraft did not extend to the upper fuselage. No 810 Sqdn converted from Sharks to Swordfish in September of 1937 and transferred to the newly commissioned HMS ARK ROYAL the following year.

A Swordfish Mk I, code 609, launches from the HMS FURIOUS during the late 1930s. A flying-off platform was placed under the forward main flight deck. No. 812 Sqdn replaced their Baffins with Swordfish in October of 1936. This unit later transferred from the FURIOUS to the COURAGEOUS. A German submarine sank the latter ship on 17 September 1939.

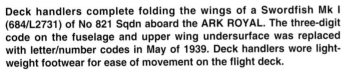

Pilots man their Blackburn Skuas at a Royal Naval Air Station (RNAS) early in World War Two. Groundcrewmen turn the propeller blades to clear pooled oil from the engine cylinders before engine start. A 30 pound (13.6 KG) practice bomb is mounted under the near Skua's port wing. The Skua was the FAA's first monoplane aircraft, having entered service in November of 1938. The Skua saw action as a dive-bomber and fighter-reconnaissance aircraft during the first two years of the conflict.

Into Action

September of 1939 proved a hard introduction for the FAA carriers, with their strength reduced by one vessel. On 17 September, HMS COURAGEOUS was torpedoed and sunk while part of an anti-submarine force. Over 500 crewmen were drowned. The following winter saw little direct carrier involvement, but the situation altered drastically with the German invasion of Denmark and Norway on 9 April 1940. With Norway out of range for RAF fighters in Britain, it fell to HMS ARK ROYAL, FURIOUS, and GLORIOUS to provide basic air cover to the Anglo/French ground forces. Carrier-based Skuas were used to attack German targets in Norway. Ironically, the Skuas that sank the German light cruiser **KÖNIGSBERG** on 10 April were from Nos 800 and 803 Squadrons based at Hatston airfield in the Orkney Islands! The limitations of the Sea Gladiator as a fighter with four machine-guns and the Skua's poor defensive armament and unarmored fuel tanks were typical of the steadily mounting odds the FAA had to contend with during the two-month Norwegian Campaign. Despite this, a steady number of Luftwaffe aircraft were downed. All three carriers managed to survive numerous aerial assaults, although a bomb-blast did force the FURIOUS to return to Britain for necessary temporary repairs. The GLORIOUS embarked the Hawker **Hurricanes** of the RAF's No 46 Squadron from Bardufoss in northern Norway during the Allied withdrawal. On 18 June, the carrier was intercepted and sunk by the German battlecruisers **SCHARNHORST** and **GNEISENAU**, with a heavy loss of life among the GLORIOUS' crew. The Norwegian Campaign was a classic example of 'too little, too late,' a situation which dogged the Allied Powers over the ensuing two years.

This Skua (L6G/L3011) was assigned to No 806 Sqdn, which was shorebased at RNAS Eastleigh, England. The tailcode indicated assignment to HMS ILLUSTRIOUS. The Sky Grey (FS36463) undersurface color was applied high on the fuselage side and on the vertical tail. The Skua had a Type B roundel (red and blue) on the fuselage, instead of the usual Type A (red, white, and blue) insignia.

FAA aircraft were camouflaged with the outbreak of war in 1939, Upper surfaces were painted Extra Dark Sea Grey (FS36118) and Dark Slate Grey (FS34096). The upper surfaces of biplanes' lower wings were Dark Sea Grey (FS36173) and Light Slate Grey (FS34159) until early 1941, when they were changed to Extra Dark Sea Grey and Dark Slate Grey. Undersurfaces were finished Sky Grey (FS36463), which was often extended to the fuselage sides and vertical tail surfaces through early 1941. The undersurface color was changed to Sky (FS34504) in August of 1940. Fuselage codes were painted black, white, Light Slate Grey, or red, depending upon the aircraft's finish.

HMS COURAGEOUS was a battlecruiser converted to an aircraft carrier and was commissioned on 5 May 1928. An aircraft – believed to be a Fairey IIID reconnaissance aircraft – was spotted on the forward flying-off deck during the early 1930s. A barrier erected across her main flight deck was a windbreak, to reduce gusts across the deck. The COURAGEOUS saw only two weeks of wartime service before the German U-boat (submarine) U-20 sank her southwest of Ireland on 17 September 1939.

Battle of the Atlantic

The initial period of the Battle of the Atlantic began in a deceptive manner, with the *Kriegsmarine* (German Navy) laboriously building up its U-boat (*unterseeboot*; submarine) strength. The Germans saw their primary threat to British merchant convoys being provided by their capital ships (battleships and battlecruisers). The armored cruiser – popularly called a 'pocket battleship' – **ADMIRAL GRAF SPEE** did sizeable destruction in the Atlantic. She was hunted down and destroyed in the River Plate off Montevideo, Uruguay in December of 1939. In this time, the FAA's main role was to seek out and destroy German blockade-runners.

The German occupation of France in June of 1940 provided access to major seaports from which the U-boats could sail directly into the Atlantic. Their crews had aerial co-operation in the form of the Focke-Wulf **Fw 200 Condor**, whose reconnaissance effectiveness was enhanced by the initial absence of effective aerial defenses. In early 1941, both the SCHARNHORST and the GNEISENAU made further effective sorties before returning to the French base at Brest. But the worst potential threat to the already hard-pressed convoy system emerged in May of 1941, when the massive battleship BISMARCK sailed from Norway out into the North Atlantic.

While the battlecruiser **HOOD** and the newly commissioned battleship **PRINCE OF WALES** sailed to intercept, the equally new carrier VICTORIOUS also entered the fray. The shocking loss of the HOOD in a brief battle off Iceland on 24 May was followed by the BISMARCK eluding her 'shadowing' cruisers **SUFFOLK** and **NORFOLK**. Swordfish from No 826 Squadron aboard the VICTORIOUS – led by Lt Cdr Eugene Esmonde – attacked the BISMARCK later on the 24th, but inflicted only minor damage on the German battleship.

The ARK ROYAL steamed up from Gibraltar and launched her No 810 Squadron Swordfish after a RAF Consolidated **Catalina** found the BISMARCK on 26 May. The airmen picked out a warship through poor visibility and launched their 'tin-fish'; however, it was not the BISMARCK, but the British cruiser **HMS SHEFFIELD**, which acted in a 'shadowing' role! Fortunately, the torpedoes' magnetic pistols impacted upon contact with the water. The Swordfish returned to the ARK ROYAL to prepare a new attack, this time with contact fuses fitted to the torpedoes. By now the carrier deck was pitching violently, but all the Swordfish were successfully launched. This time, the BISMARCK was picked out and struck by two torpedoes. The second weapon hit her rudder, irreparably jamming the massive unit and causing the warship to steam in continuous circles. All Swordfish were safely recovered aboard the ARK ROYAL, despite low visibility and rain that night. Royal Navy warships surrounded and sank the BISMARCK the next morning, 27 May.

Esmonde was also involved in the infamous 'Channel Dash' by the SCHARNHORST, the GNEISENAU, and the heavy cruiser **PRINZ EUGEN** on 11-13 February 1942. A combination of German initiative and British air and submarine reconnaissance failure allowed the German warships to slip up the English Channel from Brest, France. Esmonde's No 825 Sqdn was then based at Manston, Kent and took off to attack the vessels on 12 February. The failure of their Supermarine **Spitfire** fighter escort to rendezvous left the six lumbering Swordfish wide open to attack by Messerschmitt **Bf 109** and Focke-Wulf **Fw 190** fighters. The upper wing of Esmonde's aircraft was ripped off and the aircraft plummeted into the sea. No aircraft survived the attack and only five out of 18 airmen survived, while no torpedoes hit a target. The three warships reached Germany; however, their tactical success was a strategic failure, since they now had a much more protracted and difficult route into the Atlantic.

The U-boat threat to Britain was more consistent and lethal, but the provision of proper large-scale shipborne aircraft numbers to counter that threat was many months away in 1940-41. The initial and somewhat desperate counter-measure was to install catapults on the seaplane training ship **HMS PEGASUS** and four converted merchantmen. These modified ships – called Fighter Catapult Ships (FCS) – could carry up to three Fairey **Fulmar** fighters from No 804 Sqdn, whose primary duty was to drive away or down 'shadowing' Fw 200 Condors. Some 33 convoys were covered in this basic manner up to late 1941, but two FCS were sunk in the process. These losses included the FCS **PATIA**, which was lost before she embarked her aircraft!

The second form of catapult vessel appeared in May of 1941, with 30 'Empire' class merchantmen equipped with one bow-mounted catapult per ship. This ship type was called the Catapult Armed Merchant (CAM) ship. Each catapult bore a Hawker Hurricane fighter manned by an RAF pilot. Over the ensuing two years, the CAMs protected upwards of 20 convoys. Although just eight operational launches were recorded, these resulted in six 'destroyed' and three 'probable' claims. In both FCS and CAM operations, the British pilots had the stark choice of bailing out over the convoy or heading for friendly soil, should that latter option be attainable. The cost in vessels was high, with 13 FCS and CAM ships sunk.

The first true escort-carrier type was a conversion of the captured German refrigerator ship **HANNOVER**. The vessel was renamed **HMS AUDACITY** when commissioned into the RN on 20 June 1941. Her

Swordfish are spotted on the aft flight deck of HMS ARK ROYAL early in World War Two. The deck elevator parallel to the 'island' superstructure was lowered to the hangar deck. The ARK ROYAL and her aircraft played a prominent role in FAA activities between 1939 and 1941.

A Skua crewman adjusts his colleague's helmet while standing alongside their aircraft, with a deck crewman standing nearby. The Skua's rear gunner was armed with a .303 caliber (7.7MM) Lewis Mk IIIE machine gun. The aft canopy panel was opened for access and for firing the weapon.

short 420-foot (128 m) long flight deck supported just eight Grumman **Martlet** (**F4F Wildcat**) fighters. Only two arrestor cables were fitted and there was no hangar facility. Over the course of her short career on the Gibraltar convoy route, the AUDACITY's fighters downed at least five 'shadowers' and assisted in the sinking of U-131 while losing just one aircraft and pilot. The carrier was torpedoed and sunk by U-751 while sailing from Gibraltar on 20 December 1941.

Britain ultimately turned to 'The Arsenal of Democracy' – the United States – for a comprehensive long-term solution. British shipyards were by then fully taken up with constructing escort vessels, particularly corvettes and frigates. The first of 33 US-built escort carriers (CVEs) was the **HMS AVENGER**, which was lost in the Mediterranean following Operation TORCH (the Allied invasion of French North Africa) in November of 1942. The violent explosion from a single torpedo strike was caused by an insecure gasoline system. Subsequent delivery of the other CVEs was delayed until satisfactory modifications were introduced. The first of these modified vessels, **HMS BITER**, entered service just as the Battle of the Atlantic reached its climax. In early 1943, Britain was losing over 600,000 tons (544,320 mt) of merchant shipping per month. This was a 'break-even' figure beyond which production would fatally lag if this loss-rate were sustained. In March, two huge convoys were intercepted and lost 21 vessels, while just one U-boat was sunk. During April and May, the presence of the Iceland-based VLR (Very Long Range) Consolidated **Liberator**s of No 120 Sqdn was added to the aerial strength of both the BITER and the **USS BOGUE** (CVE-9). Also arriving on the scene was the lethal Mk 24 Mine – an air-dropped 'homing' torpedo – while the second RN escort-carrier **HMS ARCHER** appeared. The first of 13 U-boats sunk during April and May was U-203, falling to a Swordfish of the BITER's No 811 Sqdn. A No 819 Sqdn Swordfish from ARCHER so crippled U-752 that she was abandoned. Finally, U-89 was depth-charged to destruction by the escorts, after being guided to their prey by a Swordfish from the BITER.

On the Gibraltar convoy route, the aircrews on HMS BITER, **FENCER**, and **BATTLER** shared a similar cover duty along with **HMS PURSUER**. The latter warship was a specialist 'assault' carrier bearing only Wildcat Mk Vs. One action in February of 1944 against a force of Heinkel **He 177**s and Fw 200s armed with Henschel **Hs 293** 'glide-bombs' led to the interception and destruction of two bombers. By now, the FAA was operating its aircraft in a 'hunter-killer' role, using Wildcats to engage the gunners aboard U-boats remaining to fight it out on the surface. The fighters generally allowed their companion Avenger or Swordfish to deliver depth charges or rockets.

Four out of the final figure of 37 CVEs were built in Britain. These

Three Blackburn Roc fighters fly in 'vee' formation during 1939-40. The aircraft was armed with four .303 caliber machine guns in a turret. The aft fuselage spine behind the cockpit retracted to allow the gunner to fully train his weapons. The lead Roc has what appears to be a Type B fuselage roundel with a yellow outer ring.

ships were **HMS ACTIVITY**, **CAMPANIA**, **NAIRANA**, and **VINDEX**, which entered service in May of 1943. The vessels featured protection for fuel and ordnance as well as anti-fuel vapor precautions; the loss of both the AVENGER and the DASHER to similar violent explosions undoubtedly influenced Admiralty thinking. The flight decks were made of steel as opposed to the wooden decks of US escort carriers, and one hangar was provided.

The final variation in escort-carrier design was totally British – the Merchant Aircraft Carrier (MAC)-Ship. Nineteen grain-ships and oil tankers replaced their superstructures with 422-ft. (128.6 m) long flight-decks; the former vessel-type also bore a hangar facility. Two Swordfish Sqdns – Nos 936 and 869 – provided a pool of aircraft for the MAC-Ships, divided into flights of four (grain-ships) and three (oil tankers) aircraft. The ships' crews, apart from the aircrew and deck-crews, were provided by the Merchant Navy.

From May of 1943, the U-boat threat – although never totally eliminated – never remotely attained its former level for the remainder of World War Two. The part that 13 'Trade Protection' RN CVEs played in this defeat cannot be underestimated; however, the early pace of U-boat destruction by FAA aircraft generally gave way to largely non-eventful convoy patrols. On the other hand, the very presence of aircraft was of passive benefit by forcing the U-boats to remain submerged for fear of being attacked. Later in the war, the even more effective Grumman **TBF/TBM Avenger** torpedo-bomber operated off the CVE decks. FAA crews directly or indirectly sank 19 U-boats from May of 1943 until the war in Europe's end on 8 May 1945.

This Fairey Fulmar Mk I was assigned to No 808 Sqdn aboard the ARK ROYAL during 1941. This twin-seat fighter's basic shape was similar to the Fairey Battle light bomber. The Fulmar's maximum speed of 256 mph (412 kmh) was slower than most Axis fighters; however, it gave sterling service between 1940 and 1942. Fulmar pilots in the Mediterranean claimed over 100 'kills.'

A Swordfish just raised from the hangar deck warms up its engine aboard an aircraft carrier. Deck crewmen prepare to unfold its wings prior to launch. Two other Swordfish, a Fulmar, and four Skuas were spotted on the aft flight deck preparing for takeoff. Swordfish from the carriers VICTORIOUS and ARK ROYAL aided in the pursuit of the BISMARCK in May of 1941.

A Fulmar pilot (in peaked cap) and his observer check .303 caliber ammunition belts supplied by a white-capped deck crewman in a carrier's hangar deck. The upturned flap was folded over the starboard outer wing, near the machine gun bay. A tripod brace secured the folded wing to the fuselage. The Fulmar was armed with eight wing-mounted Browning machine guns in the wings, with 750 to 1000 rounds of ammunition per gun. Some aircraft also had one .303 caliber Vickers 'K' gun mounted in the observer's aft cockpit.

Deck crewmen load a 500 pound (226.8 KG) bomb onto a No 800 Sqdn Skua (6H) aboard the ARK ROYAL in 1940. The bomb was attached to a two-armed crutch under the fuselage. This crutch swung out to release the bomb away from the propeller arc. An RAF sergeant in front of the aircraft and one of the Skua's flight crewman near the folded wing observes the weapons loading process. The outer wings folded aft to reduce the Skua's wingspan aboard the carrier.

A Fulmar is launched from the ARK ROYAL on a fighter escort mission, while another Fulmar and three Skuas wait their turn. The Fulmar's canopies were opened to allow its crew to quickly evacuate the aircraft in the event of a ditching. The aircraft's starboard wingtip passes over the aft elevator. The retractable crash barrier is immediately in front of the Fulmar's wheels. This barrier was raised during recovery operations to prevent landing aircraft from overshooting into the forward parking area. A cruiser, believed to be of the County class, steams off the ARK ROYAL's port quarter.

A Fulmar has its arrestor hook lowered as it prepares to recover aboard the ARK ROYAL. The hook engaged the first of the steel arrestor cables strung across the carrier's aft flight deck. The cables were raised for recovery operations, which allowed the hook to easily grab the cable and bring the aircraft to a stop. Three deck crewman stood in the gallery beside the flight deck and prepared to assist in releasing the hook from the arrestor cable after the Fulmar had come to a stop. This Fulmar was assigned to either No 807 or 808 Sqdn, both of which operated off the ARK ROYAL during 1940 until the carrier's sinking on 13 November 1941.

Deck hands push a recovered Fulmar towards a fleet carrier's stern, where it would likely be lowered into the hangar deck for servicing. One crewman braces himself against the intake for the 1080 horsepower (HP) Rolls-Royce Merlin VIII engine. The wings were folded back after recovery, with the flaps extended. The pilot remained in the cockpit during the deck handling to work the brakes. The metal strip fitted in front of the canopy hid exhaust flames from the pilot's eyes at night and in low visibility.

In addition to carrier-based operations, several British battleships and cruisers embarked Swordfish as spotter and reconnaissance aircraft early in World War Two. A Swordfish Mk I floatplane (V4367) of No 701 Catapult Flight is lowered over the side of the battleship HMS MALAYA at Scapa Flow during 1940. The engine ran while the crew settled into their positions inside the cockpit. Paint on the floats showed wear from frequent immersion in salt water. Scapa Flow in the Orkney Islands north of Scotland was a major British naval base during both World Wars.

Swordfish of No 825 Sqdn are arranged on the flight deck of HMS VICTORIOUS, armed for an attack on the German battleship BISMARCK on 24 May 1941. The slight sea swell soon changed to heaving waters, which sent the carrier's bow through a 40 foot (12.2 м) vertical pitch prior to launch. All the Swordfish took off despite these conditions and attacked the BISMARCK, which was loose in the North Atlantic and threatening Britain's sea lanes of communication. The assault scored one hit on the battleship and all Swordfish successfully recovered aboard the VICTORIOUS.

Carrier Codes for Aircraft, 1939-41

Letter	Ship
A	ARK ROYAL
C	COURAGEOUS
E	EAGLE
F	FORMIDABLE
G	GLORIOUS
H	HERMES
L	ILLUSTRIOUS
M	IMPLACABLE
N	INDOMITABLE
R	ARGUS
U	FURIOUS
V	VICTORIOUS

Squadron Code Number Ranges

Number Range	Role
1-5	Torpedo/Spotter/Reconnaissance
6-7	Fighter
8	Fighter (later allocation)

Example: A5 was assigned to a torpedo squadron aboard ARK ROYAL, while E6 was given to a fighter squadron aboard EAGLE.

Individual Aircraft Code Letters

Letters	Flight (within Squadron)
A to C	1
F to H	2
K to M	3
P to R	4
U to W	5

Lt Cdr Eugene Esmonde (second from left) poses with four of his No 825 Sqdn colleagues in front of a Swordfish Mk I aboard HMS ARK ROYAL during the summer of 1941. Esmonde commanded the Squadron aboard the VICTORIOUS during the first torpedo attack on the BISMARCK on 24 May 1941. On 11 February 1942, King George VI presented Esmonde with the Distinguished Service Order (DSO) for leading the assault on the BISMARCK. One day later, Esmonde was killed leading six Swordfish in a vain attack upon the German warships SCHARNHORST, GNEISENAU, and PRINZ EUGEN making the 'Channel Dash' to Germany. He was posthumously awarded the Victoria Cross (VC) – the British Commonwealth's highest award for military valor, and the first awarded to the FAA – for this mission.

A Fulmar is mounted on the amidships catapult ramp of the SPRINGBANK. She was one of four merchant ships commissioned into the Royal Navy as Fighter Catapult Ships (FCS). These vessels served between December of 1940 and June of 1942, when they were replaced by escort carriers. The FCS embarked up to three Fulmars, drawn from No 804 Sqdn, which were launched to drive off or shoot down enemy aircraft threatening the convoy being escorted. The Focke-Wulf Fw 200 Condor was the primary threat aircraft these fighters faced. The FCS lacked aircraft recovery facilities, meaning that the pilot had to land on the nearest friendly airfield or ditch into the ocean.

The Fairey Seafox reconnaissance and spotter aircraft was in limited service aboard Royal Navy cruisers early in World War Two. FAA aircraft replaced their Aluminum and Cerrux Grey (FS16440) finishes with camouflage when the conflict began. Upper surfaces were Extra Dark Sea Grey (FS36118) and Dark Slate Grey (FS34096) over Sky Grey (FS36463). Upper surfaces of biplanes' lower wings were Dark Sea Grey (FS36173) and Light Slate Grey (FS34159) through 1941, while undersurfaces were Sky (FS34504) from August of 1940. This No 702 Sqdn Seafox was assigned to the Armed Merchant Cruiser (AMC) ASTURIAS, which embarked the aircraft until 1943. The aircraft was believed to be used on non-operational duties, since the aft cockpit occupant does not appear to be wearing flight clothing.

A Hawker Hurricane is launched over the bow of a Catapult Armed Merchant (CAM) Ship during a test in 1941. CAM Ships were among Britain's earliest countermeasures against the Fw 200 Condors threatening Allied convoys. A single Hurricane (usually flown by an RAF pilot) was launched to seek out and attack the German aircraft. After each mission, the pilot ditched or bailed out over the convoy or flew to the nearest friendly land. The Royal Navy used 35 CAM Ships between May of 1941 and August of 1943. The eight Hurricanes launched during this period downed six German aircraft, damaged two others, and drove off three aircraft.

A Fairey Albacore assigned to No 817 Sqdn aboard the VICTORIOUS flies past the Scottish coast during late 1941. The Albacore entered FAA service in the spring of 1940 and was intended to replace the Swordfish in the torpedo/spotter/reconnaissance (TSR) role. It was the last biplane combat aircraft to enter British service. No 817 Sqdn Albacores made an unsuccessful attack on the German battleship TIRPITZ on 9 March 1942.

A No 817 Sqdn Albacore taxis after recovering aboard the VICTORIOUS during North Atlantic operations in 1941-42. The aircraft rolls past the lowered safety barrier, which was then raised for the next aircraft to be recovered. The Deck Landing Control Officer (DLCO) on the flight deck edge has his arms stretched out to direct an incoming aircraft.

Two WRNS (Women's Royal Naval Service) personnel assist a civilian in replacing a Swordfish's canvas cockpit cover after conducting a radio test. The horizontal rods ahead of the windshield and attached to the center wing struts were torpedo sight bars with spaced lights. This sighting system was used to assess the target vessel's speed during attacks.

An Albacore's 1085 HP Bristol Taurus II engine is run up while the wings are unfolded on a carrier's aft flight deck. The wings folded aft from the fuselage joint for ease of stowage aboard all Royal Navy carriers. The items fitted under the Albacore's wings are believed to be depth charges.

A WRNS radio mechanic tests the equipment inside a Swordfish's aft cockpit. The circular fitting on the port side was a mounting point for the Type O-3 compass. Airspeed and altitude repeater indicators for the observer were placed on the port cockpit wall. Immediately aft of the observer's station was the TAG's (Telegrapher/Air Gunner) seat.

14

Royal Navy crewmen push a No 809 Sqdn Fulmar across from a Grumman F4F-3 Wildcat and three Douglas TBD-1 Devastators at RNAS Hatston in the Orkney Islands in early 1942. The US Navy aircraft were based at Hatston while their carrier, the USS WASP (CV-7), delivered Spitfires to Malta during April and May. Royal Naval Air Stations also have ship's names; for example, RNAS Hatston was titled HMS SPARROWHAWK.

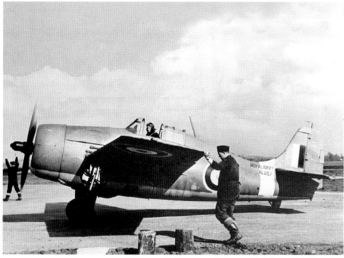

A groundcrewman holds the port wingtip of a Grumman Martlet Mk I (G-36A; AL257) taxiing for takeoff. This fighter was the 20th aircraft from the first Martlet batch. The port wing undersurface was black, which resulted in a yellow ring around the roundel. The Sky (FS34504) aft fuselage band did not extend to the undersurfaces.

Four Martlet Mk IIs (G-36B) fighters sit on the ramp at Grumman's factory in Bethpage, New York prior to delivery to the FAA. The aircraft were finished in Extra Dark Sea Grey and Dark Slate Grey over Sky. Fuselage roundels were not yet painted on these Martlets, whose wings were folded. (Grumman)

A pilot climbs into the cockpit of his Swordfish while two ground-crewmen load an 18-inch (45.7 cm) torpedo onto the aircraft. Racks under the wings were used to carry various bombs, depth charges, and flares. Swordfish were primarily used for anti-submarine operations after early 1942.

A squadron commander used the lower wing of a Gloster Sea Gladiator to spread his mission briefing map. The Sea Gladiator – a navalized RAF Gladiator fighter – was procured as a stop-gap measure in 1938. Sea Gladiators normally were equipped with a canopy, but this one was missing.

An 816 Sqdn Swordfish is raised to the flight deck of the escort carrier HMS TRACKER prior to an anti-submarine patrol over the North Atlantic. A second Swordfish is spotted aft of the elevator. An inertia starting-handle to assist in starting the engine is already fitted to the lead aircraft's forward fuselage. Swordfish on anti-submarine operations from late 1942 had white sides and undersurfaces with the Extra Dark Sea Grey and Dark Slate Gray upper surfaces.

A Swordfish assigned to No 824 Sqdn launches from the escort carrier STRIKER to join a second Swordfish on patrol in the North Atlantic. The departing aircraft was armed with a Mk 24 homing torpedo, which used a submarine's propeller noise to home in on its target. HMS STRIKER served in the Atlantic from December of 1943 until July of 1944. The STRIKER also embarked Sea Hurricane fighters; however, these were replaced by Wildcats in May of 1944.

A Sea Hurricane Mk IIC departs from the STRIKER to join two of the carrier's Swordfish on an anti-submarine patrol in the North Atlantic. The Sea Hurricanes were tasked with strafing any intercepted German U-boats (submarines) which remained on the surface. This would suppress the submarine's defenses and allow the Swordfish to effectively deliver their ordnance on the target. Swordfish crews were told to only drop homing torpedoes on submerged U-boats to prevent any reports of their existence from reaching the Germans.

Mediterranean Fortunes

Following the Italian Declaration of War on Britain and France on 10 June 1940, HMS ARK ROYAL was detached to the Mediterranean. At Gibraltar, she joined HMS HOOD (soon replaced by the battlecruiser **HMS RENOWN**) and the cruiser HMS SHEFFIELD to form Force H. The Force's function was two-fold – to challenge the Italian Fleet, and to support British operations in the Mediterranean.

In September of 1940, the newly commissioned carrier **HMS ILLUS-TRIOUS** joined HMS EAGLE at Alexandria, Egypt. In this way, pressure could be kept upon the Italians, while Force H's location at Gibraltar permitted its occasional use against German capital ships venturing into the Atlantic.

The Italians possessed a numerical and, in some cases, technically superior capital ship force. Additionally, there was the latent threat posed by the Vichy French retention of French naval units. The failure to persuade the French to sail their vessels to friendly ports resulted in the RN attacking their primary base at Mers-el-Kebir, near Oran, Algeria on 3 July. The British force included Swordfish from the ARK ROYAL, working with surface ships. After the Mers-el-Kebir attack, full attention could be concentrated on Mussolini's Navy, claiming to dominate the Mediterranean, which the Italians called 'Mare Nostrum' (Our Sea). This claim was soon to be reversed.

HMS ILLUSTRIOUS provided cover for convoys bound for the vital island of Malta, sandwiched between Sicily and North Africa. The carrier was the first to operate the Fairey Fulmar. This two-seat fighter/reconnaissance aircraft was armed with eight .303 calibre (7.7MM) machine guns and possessed a maximum speed of 280 MPH (450.6 KMH). The Fulmar's overall moderate performance did not prevent her crews giving a good account of themselves between 1940 and 1942.

Armistice Day – commemorating the end of World War One – is 11 November, but no hint of an 'Armistice' existed on the ILLUSTRIOUS' deck and hangars that evening. History was about to be made as 21 Swordfish, armed with either torpedoes or bombs, were sent against Taranto, the main Italian naval base in southern Italy. Torpedo-nets and barrage balloons protected the capital ships in the harbor. Less than an hour after the attack began, Nos 813 and 815 Sqdns had sunk the battleship **CONTE di CAVOUR** and put the battleships **LITTORIO** and **CAIO DUILIO** and the cruiser **TRENTO** out of long-term action. This was achieved with the loss of two aircraft, including that of No 815 Squadron's Commanding Officer (CO), Lt Cdr K. Williamson. The day of the aircraft carrier displacing the battleship as the primary naval weapon had arrived. The Italians transferred their other warships north

from Taranto. To this immediate tactical victory was added the psychological pressure upon the Axis Admiralties. Future sea actions would see regular vacillation by the Italians on most occasions – even when possessing a superior force.

The FAA carriers ranged across the breadth of the Mediterranean for the rest of 1940, attacking land targets and supporting convoys heading for Greece. The Germans, becoming alarmed by this degree of dominance, now stepped into the breach with the dispatch of *Fliegerkorps* (Air Corps) X to Sicily, an action that soon reaped a reward. On 10 January 1941, the ILLUSTRIOUS was disengaging from convoy escort off Malta when Junkers **Ju 87 Stuka** dive-bombers of StG (*Stukageschwaderen*; Dive-Bomber Wings) 1 and 2 descended upon her. At least six 551.1 pound (250 KG) SC250 or 1102.3 pound (500 KG) SC500 bombs struck the ILLUSTRIOUS and the battered warship barely made it into Malta's Grand Harbour. Here she lay for a further 12 days while emergency repairs were effected. A further pair of strikes from the constant aerial bombardment left her still intact and able to finally slip out and back to Alexandria on 23 January. After further patching-up, the ILLUSTRIOUS sailed for Norfolk Naval Yard, Virginia, where she remained under repair until late 1941.

HMS EAGLE served a lone function from Alexandria, before replacement by the second ILLUSTRIOUS class carrier, HMS FORMIDA-BLE. Among the EAGLE's aircraft complement was another new design, the Fairey **Albacore** torpedo bomber. Incredibly, this intended replacement for the venerable Swordfish was another biplane with fixed landing gear! Its dubious value to future FAA operations would end in a farce, since it would be phased out within two years, while the Swordfish it was intended to replace would soldier on up to V-E (Victory in Europe) Day (8 May 1945)!

The FORMIDABLE's aircrews participated in a naval action off Greece's Cape Matapan on 28 March, when the Italians sailed to intercept a Greece-bound convoy. Attacks by FAA torpedo aircraft crippled the battleship **VITTORIO VENETO** and the cruiser **POLA**. The former managed to regain her base, but the crippled cruiser, along with her detached 'escort' of fellow-cruisers **ZARA** and **FIUME**, were ambushed that night. The Italian cruisers were picked up by radar and sunk by close range gunfire from the battleships **WARSPITE**, **BARHAM**, and **VALIANT**.

Following the German invasion and occupation of Yugoslavia and Greece in the spring of 1941, the island of Crete was attacked on 20 May. Six days later, the FORMIDABLE's aircraft were attacking the airfield at nearby Scarpanto Island to indirectly relieve the pressure on Crete's defenders when the Ju 87s and **Ju 88s** of II *Gruppe* (Group)/StG 2 'Immelmann' attacked. Only two SC500 bombs hit the ship, but the

HMS ILLUSTRIOUS was the lead vessel of a six-ship class of fleet aircraft carriers and was commissioned on 25 May 1940. The ILLUSTRIOUS class had an overall length of 743 feet 9 inches (226.7 M) and displaced 28,210 tons (25,592.1 MT) at full load. Each ILLUS-TRIOUS class ship – ILLUSTRIOUS, FORMIDABLE, VICTORIOUS, INDOMITABLE, INDEFATIGABLE, and IMPLACABLE – could accommodate 36 aircraft. Swordfish from the ILLUSTRI-OUS' deck attacked the Italian fleet at Taranto on the evening of 11-12 November 1940, sinking one battleship and heavily damaging two others. (John Morrison)

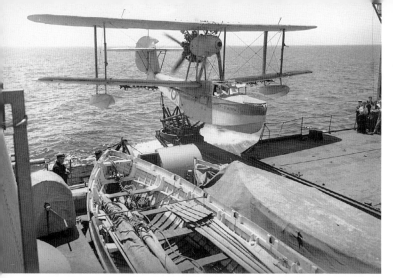

The Supermarine Walrus amphibian was primarily used as a spotter aircraft aboard battleships and cruisers. This 700 Sqdn aircraft (L2228) was being launched from the cruiser SHEFFIELD in 1941. The inscription SPOTTER OF SPARTIVENTO referred to its part in the failed bid to engage the Italian fleet off Sardinia's Cape Spartivento on 29 November 1940. (IWM)

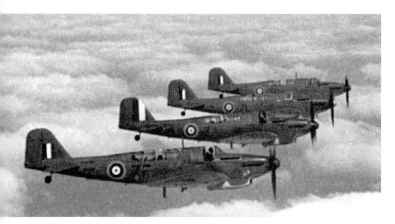

Four Fulmar Mk Is of 807 Sqdn fly in near echelon-right formation from HMS ARK ROYAL. A fin flash covers the second aircraft's entire vertical stabilizer; the three others used standard Type A markings. No 807 Sqdn flew from the ARK ROYAL from April of 1941 until the carrier was sunk that November.

Grumman Martlet Mk IIIs (F4F-3A Wildcats) assigned to 805 Sqdn are lined up at their base in Egypt's Western Desert during the latter half of 1941. Aircraft X (AX736) was camouflaged in Dark Earth (FS30118) and Mid Stone (FS30266) over Azure Blue (FS35231), with black code and serial. The Squadron operated in North Africa between July of 1941 and December of 1942.

damage was sufficient for the carrier to transit via Alexandria to the Norfolk Naval Yard for a similar long-term repair process as to her sister the ILLUSTRIOUS. The FORMIDABLE's aircraft complement then continued to operate out of Egypt, Palestine, and Cyprus with its Martlets and Albacores. The Albacores flew 'pathfinder' operations for the RAF's bombers, since the observers within each crew were expert at pinpointing targets over open spaces, whether water or desert.

The ARK ROYAL regularly embarked and launched RAF fighters intended for Malta's defense. One of her most vital contributions to the North African Campaign occurred in May of 1941. The need to get armored vehicles and aircraft to Egypt, following the heavy losses inflicted by German Gen Erwin Rommel's *Afrika Korps* was paramount. The normal route around Africa was judged to be too long in the circumstance, so the decision was taken to run convoy TIGER through the Mediterranean. On 8 May, Fulmars from Nos 807 and 808 Sqdns successfully warded off several attacks by Savoia-Marchetti **SM.79** torpedo-bombers, as well as a determined attack by Ju 88s. Only 12 Fulmars were available, but the convoy remained intact before the ARK ROYAL was forced to turn back and hand over escort duties to the FORMIDABLE. The FORMIDABLE's No 808 Sqdn downed an SM.79, two Heinkel **He 111**s, and three Ju 88s. Five of the six merchantmen reached Egypt, where they delivered 200 tanks and 43 Hurricanes. One ship was lost to a mine.

Despite their aircraft's limitations, the Fulmar crews continued to demonstrate their prowess in July when convoy SUBSTANCE was escorted. Ten SM.79s were destroyed, albeit at a cost of five Fulmars, while a high-level force of Cant **Z.1007** bombers were dispersed. (Lack of frontal armor was a probable contributory cause of the FAA fighters' loss). Up to this time, the Fairey design was the sole modern FAA British-built fighter, but in July the ARK ROYAL embarked three Hurricanes for deck-landing feasibility tests. The tests displayed the Hurricanes' poorer range and gun ammunition capabilities. The Fulmar's general performance was at least as good up to 10,000 feet (3048 M) as that for the Hurricane. For these reasons, the Fulmar retained its primary fleet fighter position for another year.

The ARK ROYAL's final convoy duty occurred in September of 1941. The carrier had made headlines ever since her first reported 'sinking' in September of 1939. Over the next two years, the German propaganda radio broadcasts by 'Lord Haw-Haw' (William Joyce) regularly asked Britain's prime minister 'Where is the ARK ROYAL, Mr. Churchill?' On 13 November, his assertions sadly bore fruit. The ARK ROYAL was hit by a single torpedo fired by U-81, after helping to deliver 300 RAF and FAA aircraft to Malta. Serious flooding ensued, but later assessments suggested that better battle-damage control procedure could have saved the vessel. Her boilers were put out of action and inoperable pumps meant that the water level rose inexorably. A true 'Legend in her Lifetime,' the ARK ROYAL sank almost within sight of Gibraltar.

Year of Crisis in the Mediterranean

The ARK ROYAL's replacement in the Mediterranean was HMS EAGLE, which along with the even older HMS ARGUS continued the supply of RAF aircraft to Malta. The two carriers also escorted merchant convoys to that increasingly beleaguered island. The presence of German U-boats in the Mediterranean during 1942 greatly increased the pressure upon the Royal Navy. In the case of the two carriers, their total fighter complement was barely adequate, although by now the majority were **Sea Hurricanes**. Standing patrols over convoy HARPOON in June resulted in a sizeable tally of 'kills' shared with the ships' anti-aircraft (AA) gunners. Sadly, most of the convoy was sunk following the carriers' withdrawal.

HMS EAGLE served in the Mediterranean during most of her wartime service. She was converted from a battleship hull and commissioned on 26 February 1924. The EAGLE's island superstructure featured her unique twin funnels. She had an overall length of 667 feet 6 inches (203.5 M), displaced 26,800 tons (24,313 MT) at full load, and could embark 24 aircraft.

Four Albacores from 826 Sqdn fly in echelon-right formation over the Western Desert in late 1941. The aircraft were based ashore after the FORMIDABLE was badly damaged by German dive bombers off Crete on 26 May 1941. The 826 Sqdn aircraft – with their undersurfaces repainted black – flew night bombing missions against German *Afrika Korps* rear positions and dropped marker flares for RAF bombers. (IWM)

The ARK ROYAL lists to starboard after a torpedo from the German submarine U-81 hit the carrier off Gibraltar on 13 November 1941. Four Swordfish cling precariously to her canted deck. Damage control problems and flooding of her boilers from the torpedo hit doomed the carrier and the ARK ROYAL sank the next day. Only one crewman died in the incident. (IWM)

19

(Above) The US loaned the carrier USS WASP (CV-7) to the British in early 1942. The WASP assisted in ferrying Spitfire fighters to Malta, which was under siege by the Germans and Italians. The carrier delivered approximately 100 Spitfires in two trips into the Mediterranean. Crewman aboard a British ship wave goodbye as the WASP returns to American waters in May of 1942. (IWM)

(Below) Supermarine Spitfire Mk V fighters are spotted on the aft flight deck of a British carrier bound for Malta during the spring of 1942. The Spitfires were equipped with Vokes tropical air filters on the engine cowlings and 90 gallon (340.7 L) external fuel tanks under the fuselage. The additional fuel enabled the Spitfires to fly approximately 660 miles (1062.2 KM) from the launching point to Malta. The carrier ARGUS and one of her escorts steam aft of the carrier. (IWM)

Operation PEDESTAL

The HARPOON and VIGOROUS supply convoys from Egypt did not deliver enough supplies to Malta in June of 1942. This failure prompted the Admiralty to order a massive merchant convoy – codenamed PEDESTAL – sent from Gibraltar with a large naval escort. The EAGLE was joined by two ILLUSTRIOUS class carriers, HMS VICTORIOUS and INDOMITABLE. The FURIOUS arrived to act as a 'ferry' vessel for Malta-bound RAF fighters. Fourteen merchantmen and 29 warships sailed from Gibraltar on 10 August 1942. On board the main carriers were 46 Sea Hurricanes, 18 Fulmars, and 6 Martlets, along with anti-submarine Swordfish and Albacores. The plan was for the Navy to provide air cover as far as the Sicilian Narrows; from there, cover would be provided by Malta-based aircraft.

The air-cover plan was seriously compromised on 11 August. The majority of the EAGLE's 20 fighters were not in the air when she received four torpedoes from U-73, rapidly turned over, and sank. Almost one quarter of the FAA fighters were removed at one stroke and no serious aerial attacks had yet been mounted. The first wave of Axis strikes occurred at dusk and with no real effect; however, several FAA fighters were fired upon by their own AA defenses upon return for landing. Several landed on the wrong carrier and at least three aircraft were 'written off' after contact with deck obstructions.

The true test for PEDESTAL occurred the next day (12 August), when three attacks involving approximately 200 Axis aircraft hit the convoy. The first of these attacks was intercepted by approximately 25 Sea Hurricanes and Fulmars, who downed four aircraft despite the presence of Bf 109 escorts. A further five Ju 88s were claimed by the inner ring of fighters over the convoy. Two Sea Hurricanes were lost, so round one fell to the Royal Navy.

A force of 100 bombers with 40 escorting fighters attacked at noon. While **SM.84**s dropped circling torpedoes ahead of the convoy, additional SM.84s and SM.79s were to deliver standard torpedo attacks. Ju 88s were to conduct bombing runs while Reggiane **Re.2001** fighters dropped anti-personnel bombs on the carrier decks. A final refinement was the presence of a radio-controlled SM.79 packed with explosives.

This complex attack plan was generally disrupted by approximately 20 FAA fighters, supported by the convoy's anti-aircraft (AA) gunners. First, the SM.84 force was intercepted well north of the convoy and held back. The Ju 88 bombers were similarly harassed and turned aside. The main torpedo-bomber force closed in on the convoy, but received a sufficient battering from the AA gunners. Only one merchantman (DEUCALIAN) was fatally damaged. The Reggiane fighters proved totally ineffective, while the radio-controlled SM.79 went out of control and crashed in Vichy French Algeria! (This was probably poetic justice, since the first Axis information on the convoy reportedly arrived via a French airliner's observation. The cloudless conditions would probably have led to equally swift disclosure to Axis reconnaissance aircraft).

The third Axis assault concentrated upon the escorts, particularly the carriers. While dusk approached, the depleted FAA 'screen' was generally overwhelmed by the Bf 109s and Ju 87s. The attackers broke through to drop two bombs upon the INDOMITABLE, which knocked her flight deck out of action. Her armored deck again proved its value in saving the vessel from total loss, although requiring long-term repair. The Fleet Air Arm had largely proved its value since the carriers and heavy warships turned back for Gibraltar. The pilots had scored a 3:1 'kill'/loss ratio. Five of the 'kills' were claimed by Lt 'Dickie' Cork. During the Battle of Britain, Cork had flown with No 242 Sqdn, whose Commanding Officer (CO) was the legendary Douglas Bader.

Now bereft of air cover, the convoy began to suffer regular losses over the remainder of its route. No less than eight merchantmen, along with

Crewmen aboard HMS INDOMITABLE gather on her flight deck prior to escorting the PEDESTAL convoy to Malta in August of 1942. The carrier carried 24 Sea Hurricanes of 800 and 880 Sqdns. Martlets of 806 Sqdn and Albacores of either 827 or 831 Sqdns are spotted on the aft flight deck. Radio antennas raised along the flight deck's edge were lowered during flight operations to allow maximum deck clearance for the aircraft. Various supply ships lie at anchor aft of the INDOMITABLE.

An 800 Sqdn Sea Hurricane (6F) is launched from the INDOMITABLE during the PEDESTAL convoy operation. An officer in white uniform beckons the pilot of another Sea Hurricane (6J) to taxi into position for takeoff. The Albacore parked on the aft port deck edge is armed with 100 pound (45.4 KG) depth charges under the wings, while the Swordfish beside it carries no external weapons. These aircraft conducted anti-submarine patrols for the Malta-bound convoys.

several escort vessels, were sunk by a combination of bombs, torpedoes, and mines. One of the five survivors, the US tanker **OHIO**, absorbed one bomb strike and a crashing Ju 87 that draped itself across her bows. Barely afloat and lashed to two destroyers, she crept into Grand Harbour fully 24 hours after three of the other four merchantmen had arrived. British service personnel and Maltese citizens lining the harbour cliff-tops greeted the OHIO in reverent silence. The supplies arrived in time to ensure the island's survival. A further late autumn convoy was necessary before long-term survival was guaranteed. By then, the British victory at El Alamein, Egypt and Operation TORCH had begun the Allied armies' pincer advance towards Tunisia and final Axis defeat in North Africa. The courage of the Allied merchant sailors surely has fewer brighter chapters than was expressed by all those involved in PEDESTAL – and on board the OHIO in particular.

(Left) A Sea Hurricane recovers aboard the VICTORIOUS, while another Sea Hurricane is spotted on the forward flight deck. She and her sister ship INDOMITABLE joined with HMS EAGLE to provide air cover for the PEDESTAL convoy. A Type 79 air search radar was mounted on top of the island's mast, with the cylindrical Type 72DM aircraft homing beacon mounted below.

(Below) Deck crewman maneuver an 880 Sqdn Sea Hurricane (7-D/AF974) on the forward elevator of the INDOMITABLE. The propeller spinner and aft fuselage band were Sky (FS34504), while Sea Hurricanes of the carrier's 800 Sqdn had black spinners with Sky fuselage bands. The Sea Hurricane lacked folding wings usually found on carrier aircraft, but were fitted with arrestor hooks and catapult spools.

(Right) Deck crewmen push an 800 Sqdn Sea Hurricane into position on the INDOMITABLE during Operation PEDESTAL. The vertical stabilizer and wing leading edges were painted flat Identification Yellow (FS33538) for recognition by the convoy's anti-aircraft gunners. The aircraft was camouflaged in Extra Dark Sea Grey (FS36118) and Dark Slate Grey (FS34096) over Sky. Two other Sea Hurricanes are spotted on the forward flight deck. A destroyer steams immediately ahead of the INDOMITABLE, with the VICTORIOUS ahead of the escort.

(Below) An 885 Sqdn Sea Hurricane is parked on the aft flight deck of the VICTORIOUS, with its pilot seated in the cockpit. Yellow recognition markings were painted on the vertical stabilizer, around the Type C fin flash. Aft of the VICTORIOUS, an Albacore gets air-borne from the INDOMITABLE while helping cover the PEDESTAL convoy. Other aircraft – Albacores, Martlets, and Sea Hurricanes – await their turn for launching. HMS EAGLE cruises aft of the INDOMITABLE.

The EAGLE cruises off the port side of either the VICTORIOUS or the INDOMITABLE in the western Mediterranean on 11 August 1942. Struts and bracing wires from an Albacore frame the EAGLE. Two Sea Hurricanes were just launched from the EAGLE when four torpedoes fired by the German submarine U-73 hit her on the port side.

The EAGLE sharply lists to port and is on fire soon after four torpedoes from U-73 hit the carrier on 11 August 1942. The carrier was approximately 65 miles (104.6 KM) south of Majorca when the German submarine attacked her. The EAGLE sank within eight minutes of being hit, taking many of her crew with her. She was the last British fleet carrier sunk in World War Two.

(Left) Personnel inspect damage caused by one of two 1102.3 pound (500 KG) bombs dropped on the INDOMITABLE on 12 August 1942. German Ju 87 Stuka dive-bombers attacked the carrier south of Sardinia. The extensive damage from this raid forced the INDOMITABLE to withdraw from the PEDESTAL convoy and retire to Britain for repairs. The Seafires spotted on the forward flight deck were not present during the German attack. Their presence on deck is surprising, considering that the carrier was unable to conduct flight operations at the time. It is believed the Seafires were hoisted aboard the INDOMITABLE, which was used to transport aircraft to British bases in the Mediterranean area.

(Below) Deck crewmen escort a recently recovered Martlet Mk II (G-36B) aboard a fleet carrier during Operation PEDESTAL. The fighter apparently suffered a collapsed tail wheel, since the deck handler directly behind the rudder guided a support trolley fitted under the aft fuselage. The few Martlets embarked on the British carriers during PEDESTAL gave sterling service, downing many of the 30 aircraft claimed destroyed by FAA pilots.

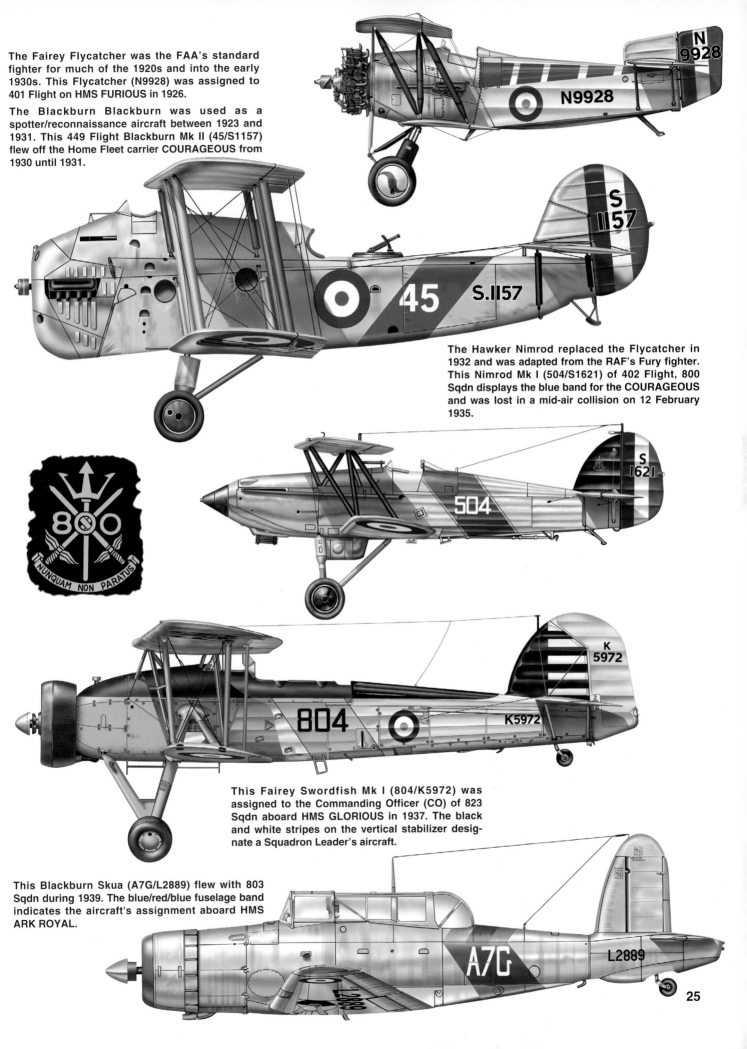

The Fairey Flycatcher was the FAA's standard fighter for much of the 1920s and into the early 1930s. This Flycatcher (N9928) was assigned to 401 Flight on HMS FURIOUS in 1926.

The Blackburn Blackburn was used as a spotter/reconnaissance aircraft between 1923 and 1931. This 449 Flight Blackburn Mk II (45/S1157) flew off the Home Fleet carrier COURAGEOUS from 1930 until 1931.

The Hawker Nimrod replaced the Flycatcher in 1932 and was adapted from the RAF's Fury fighter. This Nimrod Mk I (504/S1621) of 402 Flight, 800 Sqdn displays the blue band for the COURAGEOUS and was lost in a mid-air collision on 12 February 1935.

This Fairey Swordfish Mk I (804/K5972) was assigned to the Commanding Officer (CO) of 823 Sqdn aboard HMS GLORIOUS in 1937. The black and white stripes on the vertical stabilizer designate a Squadron Leader's aircraft.

This Blackburn Skua (A7G/L2889) flew with 803 Sqdn during 1939. The blue/red/blue fuselage band indicates the aircraft's assignment aboard HMS ARK ROYAL.

25

This Martlet Mk II is parked at Maison Blanche airfield outside Oran, Algeria after the British captured this airfield in November of 1942. The aircraft was assigned to 888 Sqdn aboard the FORMIDABLE for Operation TORCH, the Anglo-American invasion of French North Africa. The Martlet Mk II was similar to the F4F-4 Wildcat, including folding wings; however, the Martlet Mk II did not have an air scoop on the upper cowling.

Operation TORCH

On 8 November 1942, Anglo-American forces landed along the northwest shores of Africa. Aerial cover was initially provided entirely by the FAA with Sea Hurricanes and Martlets. Also on hand were the first Supermarine **Seafire** Mk IB fighters, embarked on the FURIOUS. Approximately 140 aircraft were on hand, which included Fulmars for tactical reconnaissance and liaison duties with the British Army. HMS VICTORIOUS and the recently repaired FORMIDABLE employed their Albacores for potential counter-strikes at Italian naval units, while Albacores on the FURIOUS were used for tactical strikes against land targets.

The landings proceeded swiftly despite some initial opposition and airfields were quickly secured for RAF and US Army Air Forces (USAAF) fighters. In the case of Blida airfield, Algeria, a single individual negotiated its surrender. Lt B. Nation, an 882 Sqdn Martlet pilot, sighted what he took to be a white ground sheet indicating a 'surrender' signal. Swift consultation with Rear Admiral Lumley Lyster, the British carrier commander aboard the VICTORIOUS, led to Nation's landing at Blida. Nation met the base commander, who provided him with a written note confirming the hand-over! Albacore attacks on La Senia airfield

met stiff opposition in which Morane Saulnier **MS.406** fighters and AA guns claimed four of the attackers. The Albacores nevertheless destroyed approximately 50 Vichy French aircraft.

Axis aerial involvement was minimal during Operation TORCH, although the ARGUS was hit by a Ju 88's bomb. By 15 November, the Allies' ground situation was secure and the carriers began to disperse.

On 15 December, the escort carrier AVENGER was torpedoed once by U-152 off Gibraltar. Her unmodified aviation gasoline system erupted in a monstrous explosion, from which only 17 seamen survived. An indirect form of revenge was the sinking of U-331 by a No 820 Sqdn Albacore.

Between November of 1942 and September of 1943, the Allies secured North Africa and Sicily and prepared for an advance into Italy. In that period, the Fleet Air Arm was relieved of its hitherto and largely sole responsibility for naval air cover, since it could now operate in conjunction with the RAF and USAAF squadrons. On hand for the 10 July invasion of Sicily (Operation HUSKY) were HMS FORMIDABLE and INDOMITABLE, the latter carrier recently returned from Norfolk Naval Yard. Six days after the invasion began, the INDOMITABLE was torpedoed by a Ju 88 on 16 July. The damage was severe enough to merit a second prolonged withdrawal from operational service.

A DLCO (Deck Landing Control Officer; US=Landing Signal Officer) guides a Seafire to a neat recovery aboard the FORMIDABLE. During the winter of 1942-43, this carrier returned to the Mediterranean after lengthy repairs in the United States. Three other Seafires are spotted along the starboard edge of the flight deck. The tail wheels are placed into outriggers fitted to the flight deck side, which increased the number of aircraft embarked by the carrier. The two forward parked aircraft – including White K (M3345) – are Seafire Mk IBs, each fitted with a Vokes air filter on the lower engine cowling. This filter kept sand and dust out of the engine during operations in tropical climates.

Two 885 Sqdn Seafire Mk IICs (ø-6K/MB345 and ø-6F/MB182) are spotted along the starboard side flight deck of the FORMIDABLE in the Ionian Sea following the North Africa campaign's completion in May of 1943. Their finishes displayed considerable wear from exposure to sun and salty sea spray. The fin flash on ø-6F displayed the Squadron insignia. Sailing port of the FORMIDABLE are (Left-Right): the battleships NELSON and RODNEY and the carrier INDOMITABLE.

A Seafire Mk LIIC launches from the escort carrier HMS HUNTER during Operation AVALANCHE – the US invasion of Salerno, Italy – on 9 September 1943. The HUNTER and four other escort carriers provided direct naval cover and ground support for the assault. A number of Seafires were lost due to still air conditions and the lower speed and short flight decks of the escort carriers. These conditions caused several accidents during recovery operations.

Salerno

While British Gen Sir Bernard Montgomery landed his force across the Messina Strait, a second force under US Lt Gen Mark Clark landed at Salerno on Italy's west coast on 9 September. Salerno was out of effective land-based aircraft range; fighter cover was to be assigned to the FAA. Force V consisted of the CVEs HMS ATTACKER, BATTLER, **HUNTER**, **STALKER**, and **UNICORN** lying off the beachhead. The ILLUSTRIOUS and FORMIDABLE acted as a screen against possible Italian naval intervention. (Ironically, the main Italian fleet was already sailing south to surrender to the Allies at Malta!)

The main fighter on board the CVEs was the Seafire, a Spitfire adapted for carrier operations. This fighter would serve in the dual role of cover for the troops and ground-attack. Dependence on carrier-based fighters was expected to be brief, since the seizure of Montecorvino airfield just inland was confidently anticipated within no more than 24 hours. However, Operation AVALANCHE proceeded 'according to somebody else's plan.' Axis resistance was not only more severe than expected, but there was also a grave danger over the first two days that a 'Dunkirk Evacuation' situation could arise, with the troops having to get out as best they could! Heavy naval guns helped to first stabilize and then turn the situation around; however, it was four days before the troops reached Montecorvino. The troops found a facility requiring much effort to put it back into operational condition. In the meantime, a landing strip at Paestum was prepared from which the Seafires operated until relieved by their RAF and USAAF counterparts.

The Seafire was not the best design for carrier operations, since its landing gear could not take much punishment, especially during landing. Additionally, the almost windless conditions and the short CVE decks gave little or no margin for error should a landing be misjudged.

A Seafire Mk LIIC overshoots the HUNTER on a recovery attempt during Operation AVALANCHE. Another escort carrier steams off the port quarter. Allied plans to use Montecorvino airfield on 9 September were thwarted by stiff German resistance at Salerno. An alternative airfield at Paestum was not ready for use until 12 September, three days later.

Almost all Seafires losses were due to these factors. Despite these concerns, over 200 individual sorties were flown in the first three days of AVALANCHE, although heavy ground haze generally thwarted the pilots' efforts at effective ground-support sorties.

Martlet Mk IVs (similar to F4F-4 Wildcats) of 893 Sqdn prepare to launch from the FORMIDABLE during the Salerno invasion. Seafires of 885 Sqdn are spotted to starboard of the Martlets. The FORMIDABLE and her sister ship ILLUSTRIOUS were assigned to Force H during Operation AVALANCHE. The Force was positioned between the beachhead and any likely intervention by Italian naval forces. The Italian fleet did not put up any resistance; instead, it headed towards Malta to surrender.

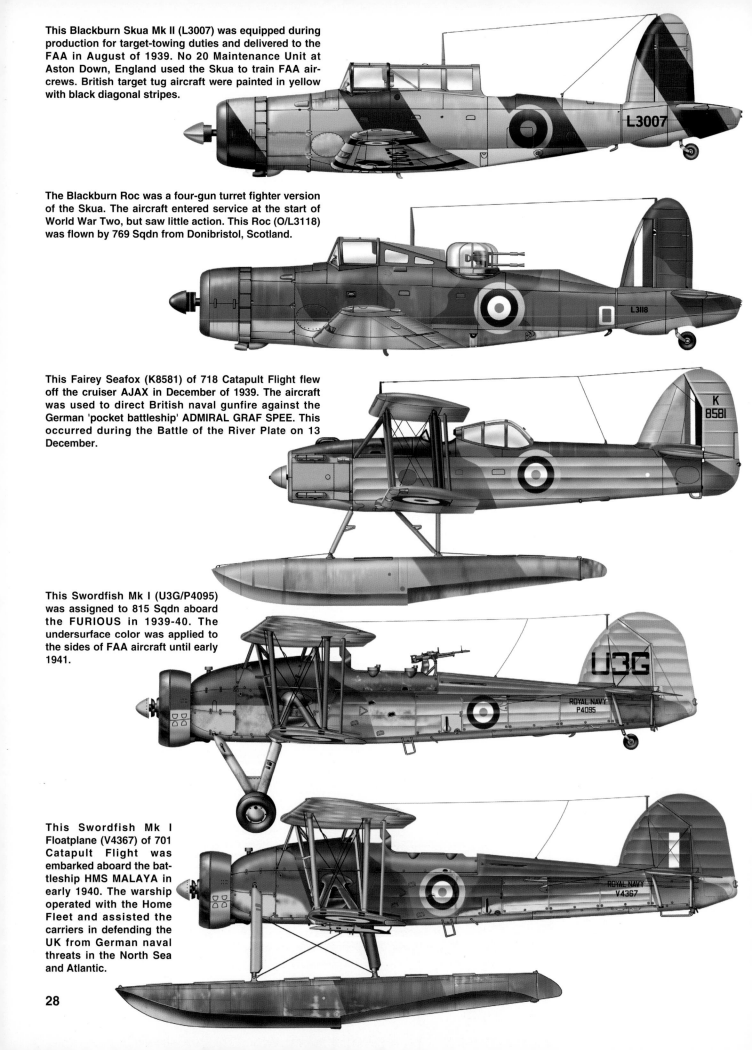

This Blackburn Skua Mk II (L3007) was equipped during production for target-towing duties and delivered to the FAA in August of 1939. No 20 Maintenance Unit at Aston Down, England used the Skua to train FAA aircrews. British target tug aircraft were painted in yellow with black diagonal stripes.

The Blackburn Roc was a four-gun turret fighter version of the Skua. The aircraft entered service at the start of World War Two, but saw little action. This Roc (O/L3118) was flown by 769 Sqdn from Donibristol, Scotland.

This Fairey Seafox (K8581) of 718 Catapult Flight flew off the cruiser AJAX in December of 1939. The aircraft was used to direct British naval gunfire against the German 'pocket battleship' ADMIRAL GRAF SPEE. This occurred during the Battle of the River Plate on 13 December.

This Swordfish Mk I (U3G/P4095) was assigned to 815 Sqdn aboard the FURIOUS in 1939-40. The undersurface color was applied to the sides of FAA aircraft until early 1941.

This Swordfish Mk I Floatplane (V4367) of 701 Catapult Flight was embarked aboard the battleship HMS MALAYA in early 1940. The warship operated with the Home Fleet and assisted the carriers in defending the UK from German naval threats in the North Sea and Atlantic.

This Skua (L6G/L3011) was assigned to 806 Sqdn aboard the carrier ILLUSTRIOUS in early 1940. The aircraft's shore base was RNAS Eastleigh, England.

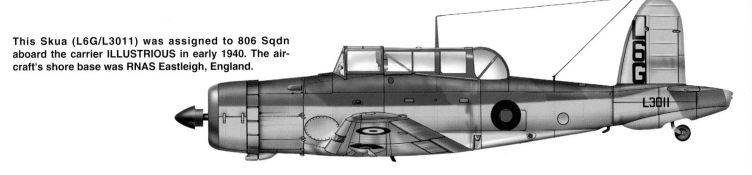

This Gloster Sea Gladiator (R/N5519) was one of four FAA machines 'borrowed' by the RAF for the Malta Fighter Flight. The flight operated from the island's Hal Far airfield in June and July of 1940. The four Sea Gladiators were Malta's sole defense shortly after Italy's Declaration of War on 10 June 1940.

Sub-Lt Parke flew this Grumman Martlet Mk I (A/BJ562) while assigned to 804 Sqdn at Skeabrae in the Orkney Islands. Parke and Lt L.V. Carter in another Martlet shot down a German Ju 88 over Scapa Flow in the Orkneys on 24 December 1940.

The fin flash – unusually – covers the entire vertical stabilizer of this Fairey Fulmar Mk I (R/N1985). The aircraft was assigned to 806 Sqdn, which was detached from the ILLUSTRIOUS to Heraklion, Crete in February of 1941.

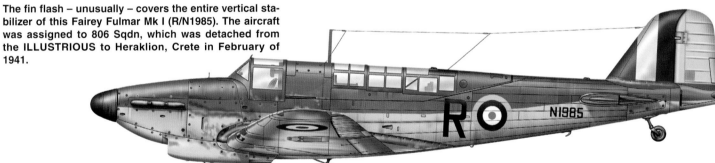

This 826 Sqdn Fairey Albacore (4K/N4424) was disembarked from the FORMIDABLE and flew from bases in Egypt during the fall of 1941. The undersurfaces were painted black for night bombing missions against Axis positions in North Africa.

(Above) Six Wildcat (formerly Martlet) Mk Vs (FM-1s) assigned to 846 Squadron (Sqdn) line up in echelon right formation during June of 1944. Aircraft from this Squadron operated from the escort carriers TRACKER and TRUMPETER in support of the Allied invasion of Normandy (Operation OVERLORD) on 6 June 1944. The Wildcats were painted with three white and two black invasion stripes – each 18 inches (45.7 cm) wide – over the standard Extra Dark Sea Grey/Dark Slate Grey/Sky camouflage finish. The serial number on the second Wildcat appears partially overpainted by striping, yet bears the same letter (D) as the formation leader.

(Below) Two 819 Sqdn personnel stand before one of their Swordfish Mk IIIs at their home base of Manston, Kent. The Squadron – part of 155 Wing, also based at Manston – laid protective smoke screens over the invasion fleet as it headed from England to Normandy. The Swordfish Mk IIIs also flew anti-submarine and sea patrol missions using the ASV Mk XI radar mounted under the forward fuselage. D-Day invasion stripes were applied over the overall black Swordfish on the evening of 4 June 1944 – two days before the assault. A unknown white cable ran along the upper fuselage side.

(Above) Aircrews from 816 Sqdn cluster around the nose of a Swordfish Mk II prior to a English Channel patrol during the summer of 1944. This variant was fitted with four rails under each wing for 3-inch (7.62 CM) rocket projectiles (R/Ps). The R/P-armed Swordfish attacked German U-boats (*unterseebooten*; submarines) and surface vessels in the North Sea. White and black Normandy invasion stripes are painted on the airframe, which had white undersurfaces and sides. The engine inertia starter handle is placed on the forward fuselage side.

(Below) This Grumman Avenger Mk II (TBM-1C) lost its port horizontal stabilizer to German anti-aircraft fire in June of 1944. This occurred during an anti-shipping raid off the French coast. The anti-aircraft fire killed the observer and wounded the pilot, Sub-Lt T.B. White, and his gunner. White managed to return his heavily damaged Avenger safely to his base in England despite his wounds and low visibility over the English Channel and southern England. The aircraft received OVERLORD invasion stripes, with a thin black border added to the rearmost white stripe.

The ILLUSTRIOUS' 810 Sqdn operated this Swordfish Mk II (2F/HS164) in May of 1942. The Squadron participated in the Allied occupation of Madagascar, including bombing missions against Vichy French positions on the island.

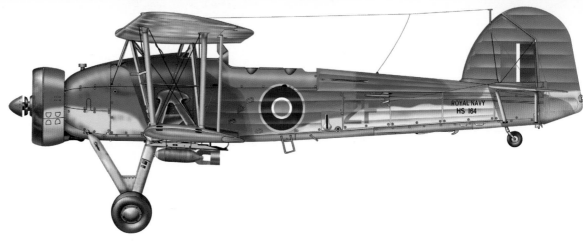

No 880 Sqdn flew this Hawker Sea Hurricane Mk IB (7-D/AF974) from HMS INDOMITABLE during the PEDESTAL convoy operation in August of 1942. Aircraft from the INDOMITABLE and other carriers helped repel Axis attacks on a large British supply convoy for Malta.

This Supermarine Seafire Mk IIC (7-B/MB240) was assigned to 800 Sqdn, which operated off the carriers ARGUS and INDOMITABLE between September of 1942 and June of 1943.

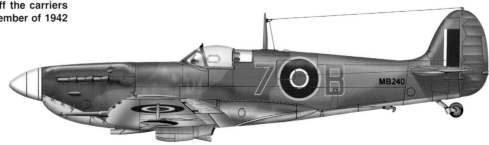

No 885 Sqdn aboard the FORMIDABLE flew this Seafire Mk II (ø6-G/MB156) during operations in the western Mediterranean in late 1942 and early 1943.

This Martlet IV (ø-7D/FN112) of 888 Sqdn operated from the FORMIDABLE during Operation TORCH in November of 1942. The Squadron insignia was applied to the port fin flash. The US-style fuselage insignia on this Martlet lacked the yellow outer ring usually applied for the invasion of French North Africa.

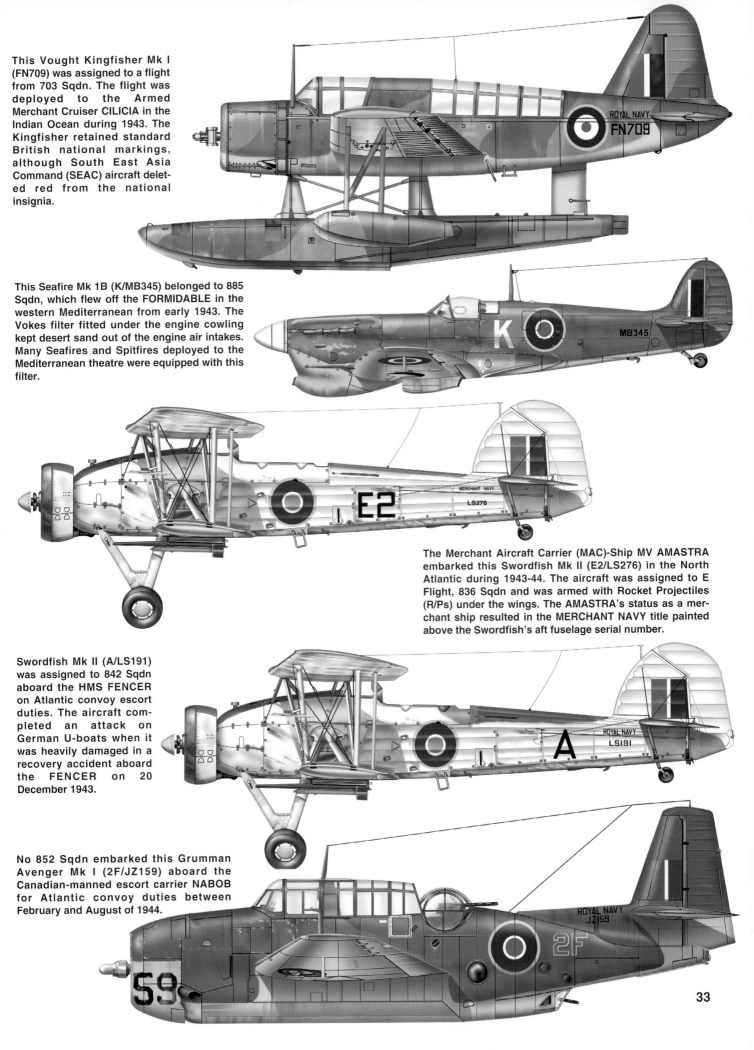

This Vought Kingfisher Mk I (FN709) was assigned to a flight from 703 Sqdn. The flight was deployed to the Armed Merchant Cruiser CILICIA in the Indian Ocean during 1943. The Kingfisher retained standard British national markings, although South East Asia Command (SEAC) aircraft deleted red from the national insignia.

This Seafire Mk 1B (K/MB345) belonged to 885 Sqdn, which flew off the FORMIDABLE in the western Mediterranean from early 1943. The Vokes filter fitted under the engine cowling kept desert sand out of the engine air intakes. Many Seafires and Spitfires deployed to the Mediterranean theatre were equipped with this filter.

The Merchant Aircraft Carrier (MAC)-Ship MV AMASTRA embarked this Swordfish Mk II (E2/LS276) in the North Atlantic during 1943-44. The aircraft was assigned to E Flight, 836 Sqdn and was armed with Rocket Projectiles (R/Ps) under the wings. The AMASTRA's status as a merchant ship resulted in the MERCHANT NAVY title painted above the Swordfish's aft fuselage serial number.

Swordfish Mk II (A/LS191) was assigned to 842 Sqdn aboard the HMS FENCER on Atlantic convoy escort duties. The aircraft completed an attack on German U-boats when it was heavily damaged in a recovery accident aboard the FENCER on 20 December 1943.

No 852 Sqdn embarked this Grumman Avenger Mk I (2F/JZ159) aboard the Canadian-manned escort carrier NABOB for Atlantic convoy duties between February and August of 1944.

33

Wildcats assigned to No 881 Sqdn prepare to launch from HMS PURSUER during the Allied invasion of southern France (Operation DRAGOON) in August of 1944. Each aircraft is armed with two 100 pound (45.4 KG) bombs under the wings for attacking German positions. The aft-facing Wildcats on the flight deck's starboard side unfolded their wings once they reached the end of the deck and were in position for takeoff. The PURSUER was the last of 11 ATTACKER class escort carriers built in the US and supplied to the Royal Navy under Lend-Lease during World War Two.

Operation DRAGOON

By August of 1944, the entire Anglo-American carrier force in the Mediterranean consisted of escort carriers (CVEs). The Anglo-American landings in southern France (Operation DRAGOON) on 15 August were intended to place further pressure upon the Wehrmacht (German Armed Forces), already desperately resisting the overall Allied advance in Normandy. Three of the original Force V units were still on hand, all operating the Seafire despite the aircraft's perceived limitations. The HUNTER and the STALKER were part of Task Group 88.2, which included the **USS TULAGI** (CVE-72) and the **USS KASAAN BAY** (CVE-69).

The other five Royal Navy CVEs in Task Group 88.1 – ATTACKER, **EMPEROR**, **KHEDIVE**, PURSUER, and **SEARCHER** – were operating Wildcats and Grumman **F6F Hellcat**s, both of which were designed and built to withstand the rigors of deck-landings and catapult take-offs.

Between 15 and 19 August, the carrier pilots made approximately 2000 individual sorties, providing close support, fleet air cover, and spotting for the naval bombardment. Few Axis aircraft contested the landings, and the sole 'kills' were registered on the 19th, when a swarm of Seafires and Hellcats downed five Ju 88s and Dornier **Do 217**s over Toulouse. The Allies lost several aircraft, but the majority of pilots were saved.

The days of active carrier operations in the Mediterranean were almost closed out after Operation DRAGOON. In September, the two Task Forces sailed into the Aegean Sea to disrupt German attempts to evacuate their island bases in the region. A process of 'sealing off' the sea routes resulted in the strafing of vessels as well as assaults on coastal defenses. Once again, carrier involvement was vital since Allied ground-based squadrons were out of range, at least until bases within Greece could be secured. The last CVE on station, HMS EMPEROR, supported a landing on Milos in the Cyclades Islands in October of 1944. The carrier's departure for Britain later that month brought down the curtain on FAA sea-borne activity throughout the Mediterranean during World War Two.

(Left) Sub-Lt B. A. Lawrence stands by his Wildcat after a ground support mission during Operation DRAGOON. His fighter hit tree tops while making an attack run against German trucks in the southern France invasion area. The trees damaged the lower port cowling edge and planted tree slivers against the engine cylinders. Lawrence was able to safely recover aboard his carrier without incident.

(Below) An 881 Sqdn Wildcat Mk VI (FM-2) is raised to the PURSUER's flight deck during Operation DRAGOON. The deck crewmen's casual clothing was prompted by the warm and sunny weather conditions in the Mediterranean off southern France in August of 1944. Several crewmen wear a variation of combat helmet liners instead of steel helmets or soft hats.

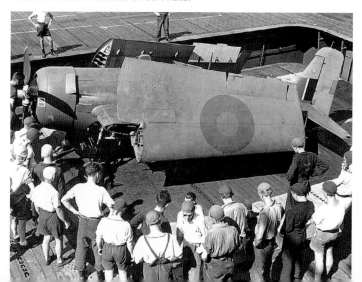

A Grumman Hellcat Mk I (F6F-3) assigned to No 800 Sqdn prepares to recover aboard HMS EMPEROR during the Allied invasion of southern France. The tail-mounted arrestor hook had just engaged one of the escort carrier's arrestor cables. The Hellcat participated in the Normandy invasion (Operation OVERLORD) the previous June and retained the white and black wing and fuselage stripes from that engagement. The FAA originally named the Hellcat the Gannet in 1943; however, the British adopted the American names of US aircraft in FAA and RAF service in March of 1944.

A Seafire LF Mk III departs from HMS KHE-DIVE on a ground attack mission against the German defenders of southern France in August of 1944. The aircraft was armed with a 500 pound (226.8 KG) bomb under the fuselage. This Seafire was assigned to No 899 Sqdn, one of three Seafire units to see action during Operation DRAGOON. The LF in the Seafire's designation stood for Low-Altitude Fighter, with an airframe optimized for low to medium-altitude flying. A 1600 horsepower (HP) Rolls-Royce Merlin 55M liquid-cooled, inline engine powered this variant. The KHEDIVE was one of 23 US-built AMEER class escort carriers supplied to the British during the war.

A US Navy F-6F-3 Hellcat is launched from HMS EMPEROR, while one of the carrier's resident Hellcat Mk Is is parked near the forward edge of the flight deck. The reason for this 'visit' during the invasion of southern France was unknown. The F6F-3 came from either the USS TULAGI (CVE-72) or the USS KASAAN BAY (CVE-69). Both American escort carriers was assigned to Task Group 88.2, which provided some of the air cover for Operation DRAGOON. The British Hellcat was assigned to No 800 Sqdn

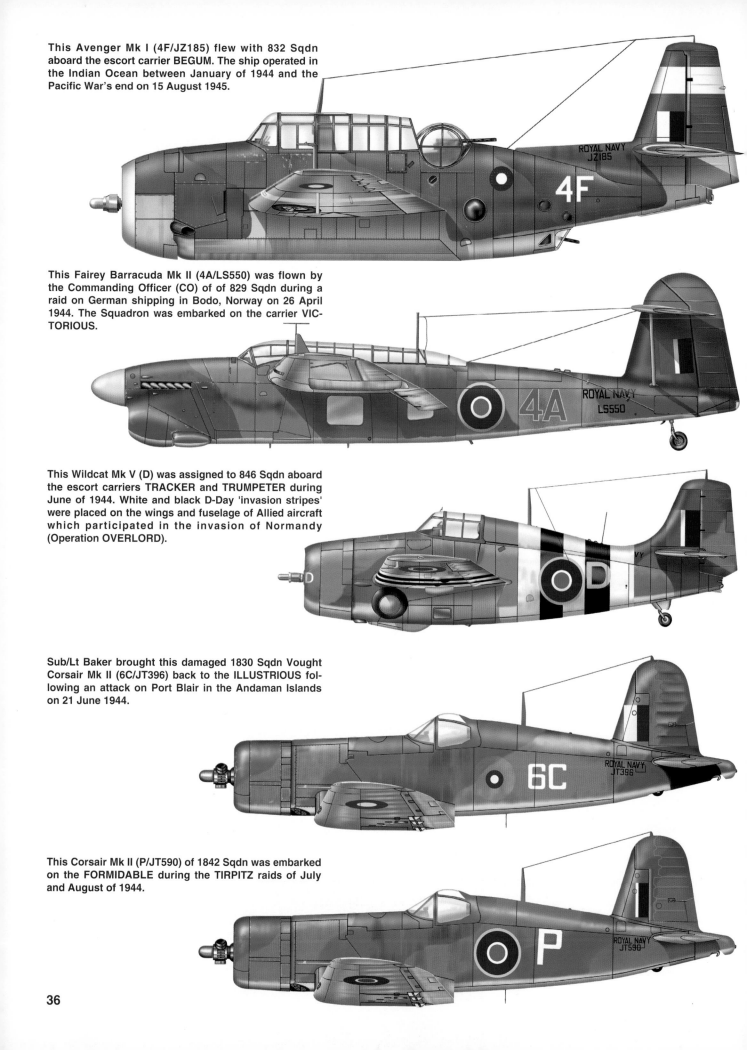

This Avenger Mk I (4F/JZ185) flew with 832 Sqdn aboard the escort carrier BEGUM. The ship operated in the Indian Ocean between January of 1944 and the Pacific War's end on 15 August 1945.

This Fairey Barracuda Mk II (4A/LS550) was flown by the Commanding Officer (CO) of of 829 Sqdn during a raid on German shipping in Bodo, Norway on 26 April 1944. The Squadron was embarked on the carrier VIC-TORIOUS.

This Wildcat Mk V (D) was assigned to 846 Sqdn aboard the escort carriers TRACKER and TRUMPETER during June of 1944. White and black D-Day 'invasion stripes' were placed on the wings and fuselage of Allied aircraft which participated in the invasion of Normandy (Operation OVERLORD).

Sub/Lt Baker brought this damaged 1830 Sqdn Vought Corsair Mk II (6C/JT396) back to the ILLUSTRIOUS following an attack on Port Blair in the Andaman Islands on 21 June 1944.

This Corsair Mk II (P/JT590) of 1842 Sqdn was embarked on the FORMIDABLE during the TIRPITZ raids of July and August of 1944.

This Grumman Hellcat Mk I (E-W/JV146) of 800 Sqdn participated in Operation DRAGOON in August 1944. The Squadron – previously employed on Operation OVERLORD – was embarked on the EMPEROR.

This Fulmar Mk IINF (BO I/BP791) flew with 784 Sqdn, a Night Fighter Training unit, from September of 1944 until June of 1945. The Squadron deployed several Fulmar night fighters to several escort carriers. The nose art depicts a black cat with a bell under the name RINGA.

No 832 Sqdn flew this Avenger Mk II (1B-K /JZ512) from the HMS BEGUM during late 1944 and early 1945. The carrier was assigned to the East Indies Fleet for operations against Japanese installations in Malaya.

This Fairey Firefly FR.I (N-278/MB444) was assigned to 1771 Sqdn, which was embarked on the IMPLACABLE. The carrier served with the British Pacific Fleet throughout most of 1945.

This 804 Sqdn Hellcat Mk II (6K-K/JV316) operated from several East Indies Fleet escort carriers from January of 1945 until the war's end. The fighter retained the standard fin flash with the SEAC (Southeast Asia Command) roundels.

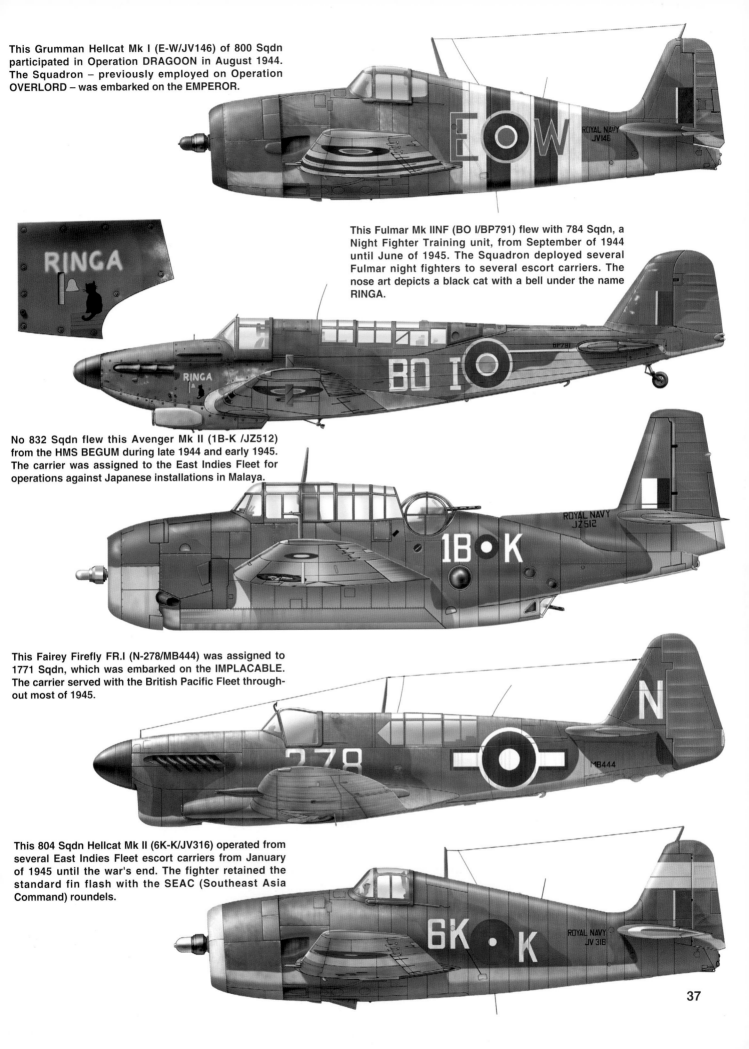

Life-Line to Russia

No sooner had Hitler invaded the Soviet Union on 22 June 1941 than Britain (followed by America in December) organized supply convoys to ease the pressure on the initially hard-pressed Soviet armies. The sea route skirted Norway's North Cape before heading east to Archangel and Murmansk. The first six convoys were virtually free of loss, probably due to German over-confidence that such an effort would be too late to materially stem the swift pace of their advance to final victory on the *Ostfront* (Eastern Front).

The initial FAA involvement was indirect, with HMS VICTORIOUS the sole fleet carrier available and her aircrews mainly attacking targets in Norway. One of the first such strikes proved most expensive. The ports of Kirkenes and Petsamo were assumed to contain much shipping and the Albacore crews were dispatched accordingly. The arrival of a 'shadowing' He 111 during the launch destroyed any chance of surprise. Worse still was the presence over Kirkenes of Bf 109s and **Bf 110**s, whose pilots downed 11 of the 20 lumbering torpedo-planes from Nos 827 and 828 Sqdns. Several Fulmar escorts also failed to return. Worse still, this effort was all for nothing, since the 'mass of shipping' did not exist. Several subsequent attacks in the region bore better results, with several merchantmen sunk and damage inflicted on industrial plants.

Direct FAA support for the PQ/QP convoys between Iceland and Archangel, Russia was then totally absent until August of 1942, when HMS AVENGER rendezvoused with PQ18 (the 18th convoy from Iceland to Archangel). She embarked 12 Hurricanes Mk IBs with a further six dismantled aircraft in her hangar deck. This barely adequate force would be challenged by superior numbers of He 111s and Ju 88s.

No attacks developed between 9 and 12 August, when the inexperience of the pilots from Nos 802 and 883 Sqdns was revealed. The appearance of several 'shadowing' Blohm und Voss **Bv 138**s led to a wholesale tail-chase. The convoy was now open to unimpeded assault, duly delivered by the He 111 torpedo-bombers that destroyed eight vessels in a single mission. Such ill discipline was not repeated and subsequent waves of attackers were successfully broken up. Also on hand was the CAM (Catapult Armed Merchant)-Ship **EMPIRE MORN**. On 17 August, her Hurricane went up and destroyed three **He 115** float-planes as well as driving off several other marauders. The pilot then headed east 200 miles (321.9 км) to land near Archangel. A further five merchantmen were lost, but the out-numbered pilots had claimed nearly 40 'kills.' Whatever the reason, the Luftwaffe never again mounted a concerted assault against a Russia-bound convoy.

The convoy system was suspended in March of 1943; however, this was cancelled late that year and CVEs provided regular convoy escort. In February of 1944, **HMS CHASER** embarked the rocket-firing Swordfish and Wildcats of No 816 Sqdn. One of the former type so damaged U-472 that she could not submerge and she was finished off by convoy escorts on 4 March. The next day, a rocket-spread sank U-366. On 6 March, U-873 was obliterated by another Swordfish rocket-barrage. This rate of interception, let alone destruction, was amazing, given that hundreds of hours of fruitless patrolling was the norm in World War Two! Additionally, the sturdy construction of the Wildcat lent itself admirably to operations off the short CVE decks, which in turn cut down the attrition rates on both aircraft and spare parts compared to other, less robust FAA aircraft.

The CHASER's success rate in sinkings was exceeded by the FENCER's No 842 Sqdn in May. The depth charges dropped by its Swordfish destroyed U-277, U-674, and U-959 – all within 48 hours (2-3 May)! Before the year's end, at least five more U-boats were lost directly or indirectly as a result of aircraft attack.

(Left) HMS AVENGER was the first custom-built escort carrier to enter Royal Navy service. Six of her Sea Hurricanes are spotted on her flight deck, which is painted in camouflage colors to confuse enemy reconnaissance and bomber aircraft crews. The AVENGER's Sea Hurricanes inflicted heavy casualties among the German torpedo-bombers, which attacked the Russia-bound Convoy PQ18 in September of 1942. She was torpedoed and sunk by the German submarine U-155 off Gibraltar on 15 December 1942.

(Below) An Albacore flipped upside-down on the flight deck of a British carrier in the North Sea, while some of the ship's personnel gather around the aircraft. The reason for this accident was unknown; however, the folded wings confirmed that this incident did not occur while the Albacore was flying! Two other Albacores are spotted on the aft edge of the flight deck.

(Above) The VICTORIOUS lies at anchor along the steep and rocky shore of Spitzbergen Island during the fall of 1941. Two 809 Sqdn Fulmars and an 817 Sqdn Albacore are spotted on the VICTORIOUS' flight deck. Spitzbergen is located approximately 600 miles (965.6 KM) north of Norway, within the Arctic Circle. On 25 August 1941, British commandos successfully raided the island's coal installations, which prevented the coal from falling into German hands.

(Below) Several 832 Sqdn Albacores are parked on the aft flight deck of the VICTORIOUS while she is moored off Spitzbergen in the fall of 1941. A Fulmar is spotted immediately aft of the torpedo-bombers. The carrier's two Albacore squadrons (817 and 832) attacked the harbor and coastal installations in Bodo, Norway on 12 September 1941. The British sank two merchant ships and moderately damaged shore facilities without any loss.

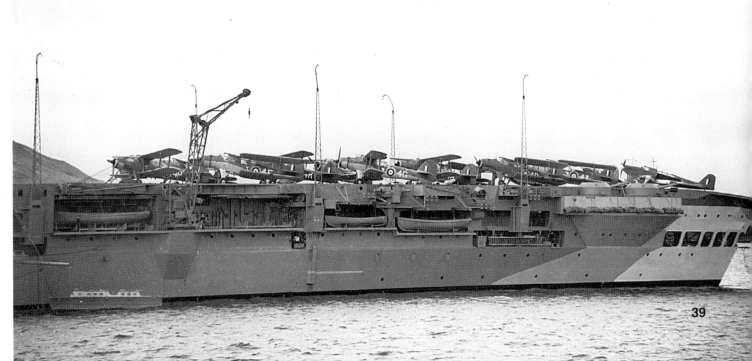

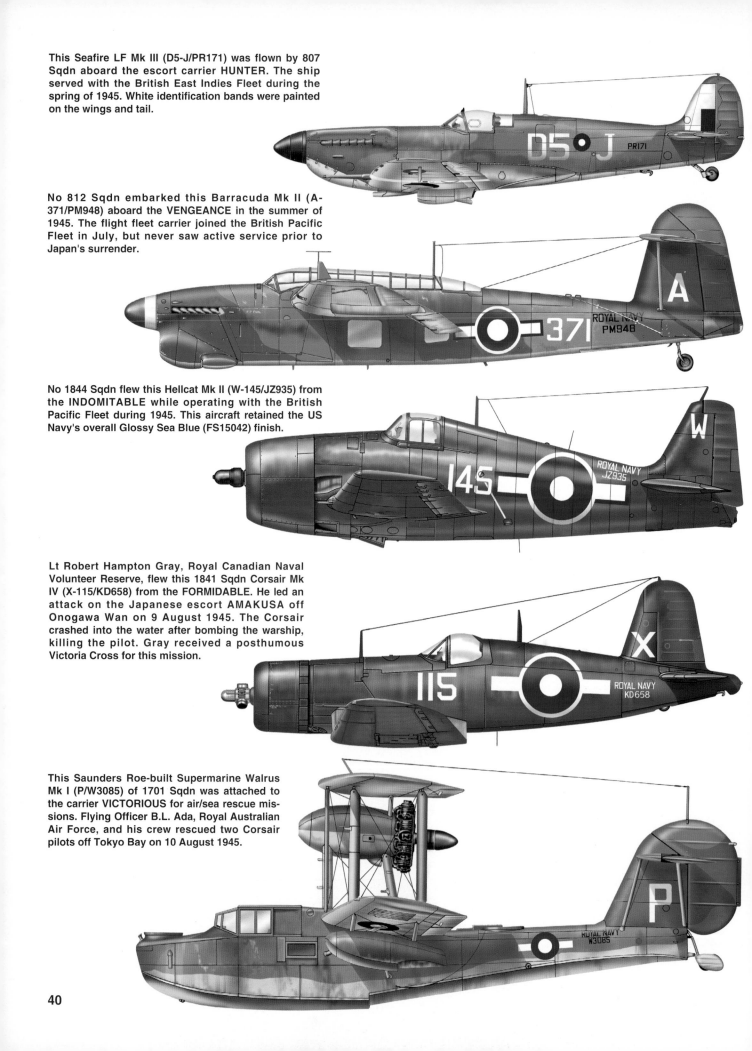

This Seafire LF Mk III (D5-J/PR171) was flown by 807 Sqdn aboard the escort carrier HUNTER. The ship served with the British East Indies Fleet during the spring of 1945. White identification bands were painted on the wings and tail.

No 812 Sqdn embarked this Barracuda Mk II (A-371/PM948) aboard the VENGEANCE in the summer of 1945. The flight fleet carrier joined the British Pacific Fleet in July, but never saw active service prior to Japan's surrender.

No 1844 Sqdn flew this Hellcat Mk II (W-145/JZ935) from the INDOMITABLE while operating with the British Pacific Fleet during 1945. This aircraft retained the US Navy's overall Glossy Sea Blue (FS15042) finish.

Lt Robert Hampton Gray, Royal Canadian Naval Volunteer Reserve, flew this 1841 Sqdn Corsair Mk IV (X-115/KD658) from the FORMIDABLE. He led an attack on the Japanese escort AMAKUSA off Onogawa Wan on 9 August 1945. The Corsair crashed into the water after bombing the warship, killing the pilot. Gray received a posthumous Victoria Cross for this mission.

This Saunders Roe-built Supermarine Walrus Mk I (P/W3085) of 1701 Sqdn was attached to the carrier VICTORIOUS for air/sea rescue missions. Flying Officer B.L. Ada, Royal Australian Air Force, and his crew rescued two Corsair pilots off Tokyo Bay on 10 August 1945.

40

No 817 Sqdn Albacores carry a mixture of 18-inch (45.7 CM) torpedoes and (aircraft 5A and 5F) A Mk I 'cucumber' sea mines. The mines were released from the aircraft either with or without a parachute to slow their rate of descent. The A Mk I was effective to a minimum depth of 30 feet (9.1 M). The nose art immediately aft of the engine cowling on aircraft 5C appeared to be a female 'pin-up.' Such personal aircraft decoration was officially discouraged and seldom seen on FAA aircraft. The Type C1 fuselage roundel and Type C fin flash and underwing roundel were introduced during the spring of 1942.

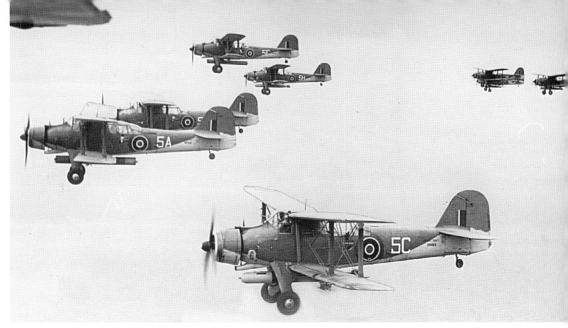

Personnel from 817 Sqdn gather around two of the unit's Albacores (including 5B/X9015) at Hatston airfield in the Orkney Islands during the spring of 1942. The Squadron was based at Hatston while its carrier, HMS VICTORIOUS, was docked at nearby Scapa Flow. An unknown kind of nose art appeared immediately aft of 5B's engine. The 5 in the fuselage code indicated a torpedo/spotter/reconnaissance (TSR) squadron aboard a carrier, while the B indicated an aircraft of the squadron's first flight. Code letters identifying carriers – for example, Y for the VICTORIOUS – were not used for much of the war as a security measure.

A WRNS (Women's Royal Naval Service) technician lowers the radio gear from an Albacore to a Petty Officer at HMS ARIEL, a FAA training establishment. She is positioned in the aft gunner's cockpit, with the hatch opened aft. A hatch for the dinghy storage is located immediately aft of the rear gunner's cockpit. The open doorway on the port fuselage side led into the cockpit. WRNS personnel – nicknamed 'Wrens' – performed maintenance and clerical duties for FAA units during World War Two, which freed men for combat duty.

(Above) FAA flight and ground crews head to their Swordfish during training at a Royal Naval Air Station (RNAS). Two of the Swordfish are fitted with dual controls and have a headrest built immediately aft of the second cockpit, which replaces the observer's and telegrapher/air gunner's posts. The aircraft are arranged as if on a carrier's flight deck prior to engine start for an immediate launch at sea.

(Below) Torpedo-armed Swordfish are lined up on the ramp at RNAS Hatston (HMS SPARROWHAWK), Orkney Islands in early 1942. Practice weapons are fitted to the aircraft for use in training exercises around the Orkneys and northern Scotland. Hatston also hosted aircraft whose carriers were berthed at Scapa Flow. A Percival Proctor communications aircraft and a Blackburn Skua are parked aft of the Swordfish near the water.

(Above) A Swordfish Mk II (HS228) converted to have dual flight controls rests between missions at a Royal Naval Air Station during 1943. Several Swordfish were converted to serve as pilot conversion trainers during the war. The student pilot sat in the front cockpit, ahead of the instructor. A Proctor communications aircraft is departing from the airfield.

(Below) A Swordfish crew runs pre-flight checks – and possibly pose for the camera – before launching from HMS BATTLER on an anti-submarine mission during 1944. The TAG (Telegrapher/Air Gunner) aimed his .303 caliber (7.7MM) Vickers 'K' machine gun, which was fitted to a Fairey High Speed Gun Mounting. The observer sighted through the compass mounted on the starboard mounting post. The pilot busied himself with his pre-flight checks.

(Above) Four Sea Hurricanes, a Fulmar, and a Seafire are attended to in the hangar deck of the carrier ARGUS during 1943. These fighters were from No 768 Sqdn, a FAA training unit based at Macrihanish, Scotland. The Squadron deployed several aircraft for shipborne training aboard the ARGUS, which operated in the Firth of Clyde along Scotland's west coast. The Sea Hurricane was armed with eight wing-mounted .303 caliber (7.7MM) machine guns.

(Below) Deck handlers push a Seafire Mk IB (M2-Y) onto the elevator of the ARGUS in 1943. One handler pulls on the propeller blade while his colleagues wheel the fighter out of the hangar deck. The Seafire was then raised to the flight deck for a training mission. Wheel chocks were placed on the starboard wing leading edge and root. Worn paint indicated the Seafire's heavy use in training fighter pilots on carrier operations.

(Above) The DLCO (Deck Landing Control Officer) gives the 'cut engine and land' signal to a Swordfish Mk II recovering aboard the TRACKER following an anti-submarine patrol in 1944. Lowered leading edge slats on the upper wing helped control the aircraft during landing, while the arrestor hook was lowered for engaging the arrestor cables on deck. The 3-inch (7.62 CM) rocket projectiles (R/Ps) under its wings indicated that no German submarines were spotted on this mission.

(Below) A Swordfish's pilot begins exiting his aircraft after recovering aboard the TRACKER in 1943. The faces of the observer and Telegrapher/Air Gunner (TAG) waiting to get out displayed the weariness of long convoy escort missions above the North Atlantic and Arctic waters. Swordfish crews often flew six-hour long missions in their open-cockpit aircraft to defend convoys from the German U-boat threat.

A Swordfish is raised up to the flight deck of a Merchant Aircraft Carrier (MAC)-Ship on North Atlantic patrol. The aircraft's folded wingspan of 17 feet 3 inches (5.3 M) was just enough to fit on this elevator. Another aircraft was parked ahead of the deck elevator. This unidentified ship was one of six grain carriers converted to MAC-Ships during World War Two. These vessels were equipped with one deck elevator mounted on the aft flight deck area. The MAC-Ships supplemented the escort carriers on North Atlantic and Arctic convoy runs. (IWM)

A Swordfish pilot prepares to recover aboard the escort carrier SMITER while another Swordfish launches from the ship. The US-built AMEER class escort carrier was used to train Deck Landing Control Officers (DLCOs) late in the war. The SMITER'S DLCO extended round white paddles from each arm to guide the aircraft on final approach and landing. The flight deck measured 438 feet (133.5 M) in length and 88 feet (26.8 M) in width.

Deck crewman prepare for launching a Swordfish Mk II from HMS FENCER's snow-covered deck during a Russian convoy operation in early 1945. Allied convoys bound to and from the Soviet Union faced constant cold and foul weather. The skies above the Arctic Circle were dark for six months and light the rest of the year. Swordfish from No 842 Sqdn aboard the FENCER sank four U-boats during the conflict, including three submarines destroyed while escorting the RA59 convoy between 2 and 3 May 1944.

This Fulmar Mk IINF night fighter (BOI/BP791) was assigned to No 784 Sqdn aboard the escort carrier CAMPANIA between September of 1944 and March of 1945. The carrier primarily escorted convoys to and from the Soviet Union. The Fulmar Mk II's tropical air filters on the side engine intakes distinguished this variant from the earlier Fulmar Mk I. RINGA in white appeared above a black cat painted on the aft engine cowl section.

Various FAA aircraft are stored in the hangar of the US-built escort carrier RAVAGER. The ship was primarily used as a training carrier during her wartime service. A Grumman Hellcat is parked across from a Fairey Fulmar Mk II and aft of another Fulmar. Two Grumman Avengers are spotted aft of the Hellcat, while a Fairey Barracuda is positioned beside the Avengers. Other aircraft are stored in the aft end of the hangar deck. RAVAGER and her sisters could accommodate 20 aircraft.

Spotter aircraft aboard Royal Navy battleships and cruisers aided the FAA carriers in observing attacks and performing search and rescue missions for downed aircrews. A lieutenant perched on the canopy supervises a Petty Officer and two Ordinary Seamen as they paddle a Walrus (S/X9586) in an Icelandic fjord in 1943. The spotter aircraft was assigned to the cruiser BELFAST, whose crane lifted the Walrus aboard after it was paddled to the ship. A white and red Rear Admiral's flag was painted on the nose, just under the bow gunner's compartment.

The TIRPITZ

One of German *Führer* (Leader) Adolf Hitler's constant phobias was an Allied invasion of Norway. He maintained a huge Wehrmacht force to counter this threat. For the British, Norway represented a more solid maritime threat, since the stationing of *Kriegsmarine* (German Navy) capital ships along its coastline had to be countered. This entailed the tying down of a sizeable naval counter-force at Scapa Flow in the Orkney Islands to ensure that the Atlantic lifeline was free of the German warship threat. From June of 1941, the threat was extended to the convoy route to and from the northern Soviet Union.

One specific capital ship dictated Admiralty thinking for upwards of three years, during which time she ironically saw no action. The battleship **TIRPITZ**, launched in 1939, was transferred to Trondheim in January of 1942. When she was joined in February by the 'pocket-battleship' **ADMIRAL SCHEER** and the PRINZ EUGEN, the Royal Navy prepared for another 'break-out' similar to that made a year before by the TIRPITZ's sister, the BISMARCK. The VICTORIOUS was operating off Tromso when the ADMIRAL SCHEER and the PRINZ EUGEN were reported steaming north. An attempted interception by 18 Albacores failed due to bad weather conditions, but the submarine **HMS TRIDENT** had better luck by heavily damaging the PRINZ EUGEN close to Trondheim on 23 February.

A second sortie by the Albacores on 9 March was even more disappointing. The TIRPITZ came out, but headed back following the failure of 'shadowing' German aircraft to pick out Allied convoys PQ12 and QP8. A miscalculation of the warship's position when the FAA crews finally broke cover left them above instead of ahead of their target. The resultant torpedo-runs by the Albacores with their fixed landing gear left the TIRPITZ with ample time to maneuver. No hits were secured at a cost of two out of the 14 aircraft.

Almost two more years elapsed before the TIRPITZ was selected for aerial attack. (Midget submarines had inflicted damage in September of 1943). By coincidence, the VICTORIOUS was again on hand when the first of several assaults (Operation TUNGSTEN) was made on 3 April. By this stage the Albacores had been displaced by Fairey **Barracuda**s, monoplane-configured dive-bombers, capable of carrying a 1600 pound (725.8 KG) armor-piercing bomb. The VICTORIOUS and the FURIOUS embarked 43 Barracudas between them. The first wave caught the TIRPITZ as she was maneuvering out to begin extended sea trials; this was a bit of good fortune for the FAA crews, since the trials were originally planned for the day before! The Hellcat and Wildcats deflected the AA gunners' aim as the 'Barras' went in to deliver their ordnance. Barely had the first wave dispersed when the second arrived to inflict further serious damage. Fourteen strikes were recorded and over 400 sailors were killed.

Two further assaults were mounted in July and August with a single 1600 pound bomb actually penetrating the deck armor – but failing to detonate! It was to fall to the RAF Bomber Command to finish off the TIRPITZ with their aerodynamic 12,000 pound (5443.2 KG) 'Tallboy' bombs. Even this process extended over three occasions before the massive warship was caught without fighter cover or smoke-float protection on 12 November 1944. The TIRPITZ rolled over at her berth in Tromso after suffering several 'Tallboy' hits.

Pilots with a variety of footwear walk past Vought Corsair Mk IIs (F4U-1D) of either 1834 or 1835 Sqdn aboard the VICTORIOUS on 3 April 1944. These men had flown the first of a series of attacks against the German battleship TIRPITZ in Norway's Alten Fjord. The near Corsair lacks patches over the starboard machine gun apertures. These patches kept cold Arctic air from freezing the gun mechanisms. (IWM)

Barracuda aircrews that attacked the TIRPITZ pose before one of their aircraft aboard the VICTORIOUS following the 3 April 1944 raid. Four depth charges are mounted on the wing racks for use against any submerged U-boats in the carrier's vicinity. The Barracudas scored 14 bomb hits on the TIRPITZ, which was forced out of service for three months.

A Seafire L Mk IIC of either 801 or 880 Sqdn is prepared for a Combat Air Patrol (CAP) mission from the FURIOUS during the raid on the TIRPITZ. Perforated wind deflector shields were raised to prevent the aircraft from being buffeted by the wind. One of the deck handlers apparently removed the wheel chocks from the landing gear, while the Seafire's pilot stands by the rudder.

HMS FURIOUS plows through strong running seas late in World War Two. The raised radio antennas along the flight deck edges indicated no flight operations were underway. From 1922 until 1925, she was refitted with a flush flight deck replacing the fore and aft decks separated by the battle cruiser superstructure. The FURIOUS saw active service throughout most of the war, most notably during the 1944 strikes against the TIRPITZ in northern Norway. She was removed from active service in September of 1944 and scrapped after the conflict ended.

Deck handlers aboard the VICTORIOUS complete putting out an engine fire from a Barracuda damaged during the TIRPITZ attack on 3 April 1944. The engine was hit by German anti-aircraft fire, yet the aircraft managed to return to its carrier. The Barracuda struck the safety barrier on recovery, which resulted in the oil cooler and engine cooler radiator being sheared off. The FAA lost two 'Barras' in the first attack on the German battleship.

An 882 Sqdn pilot climbs out of his Wildcat Mk V (S-J/JV472) after recovering aboard the SEARCHER following Operation TUNGSTEN – the 3 April 1944 attack on the TIRPITZ. Deck hands eagerly waited to hear the pilot's account of the raid. The escort carriers SEARCHER and PURSUER sent Wildcats to escort the strike force and to suppress German anti-aircraft defenses in the Alten Fjord.

A Barracuda taxis forward after returning to her carrier after attacking a German convoy off Bodo, Norway on 26 April 1944. Some FAA aircraft sank three supply ships in the convoy, while others attacked shipping in Bodo harbor. Another Barracuda and several Corsairs are spotted on the forward flight deck.

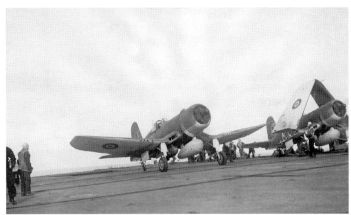

Sub-Lt L.J. Journing adjusts his parachute harness before entering the cockpit of his Barracuda on 6 May 1944. His bomber participated in attacks on German convoys off Kristiansund, Norway. The aircraft was armed with an 18-inch (45.7 CM) torpedo under the fuselage; Barracudas seldom carried this weapon in service. Barracuda main landing gears retracted up to rest inside the lower wings and fuselage sides.

A Corsair Mk II fitted with a 1000 pound (453.6 KG) bomb and a 175 US gallon (662.4 L) fuel tank prepares to launch a strike against the TIRPITZ in August of 1944. On 22-24 August, FAA aircraft conducted the final series of carrier-borne raids on the battleship, codenamed Operation GOODWOOD. Each wingtip on FAA Corsairs was clipped eight inches (20.3 CM) to fit inside the hangar decks of British carriers.

A 1841 Sqdn Corsair Mk II prepares to launch from a British carrier to escort the strike force sent against the TIRPITZ. Other Corsairs are prepared to follow the lead fighter into the air. The fighters are fitted with 175 gallon center line fuel tanks to increase their range. Humid air was likely responsible for the propeller vortices that swirled around the lead Corsair.

The pilot of this Corsair Mk II (P/JT590) begins folding his wings after recovery aboard a fleet carrier on 4 April 1944. German anti-aircraft fire damaged the starboard horizontal stabilizer and elevator, yet the pilot was able to recover safely. The Corsair is believed to be assigned to 1842 Sqdn on the FORMIDABLE – one of four Corsair squadrons deployed for Operation TUNGSTEN.

A Hellcat Mk I launches from HMS EMPEROR while three additional Hellcats await their turn during an anti-shipping mission off Norway in 1944. A 150 US gallon (567.8 L) fuel tank is mounted under each fighter's fuselage. Fighters from the EMPEROR flew cover for the initial British carrier raids on the TIRPITZ in April of 1944.

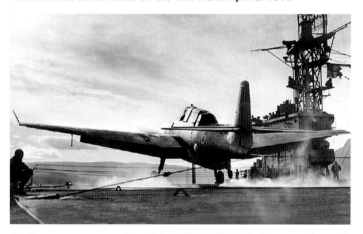

An Avenger recovers aboard the TRUMPETER during operations off the Norwegian coast in August of 1944. Smoke rises from the sudden contact of rubber tires against the wooden flight deck as the aircraft decelerates from 78 knots (89.8 MPH/144.5 KMH) to zero. The arrestor hook grabbed one cable and pulled it forward as the Avenger stopped.

Two Avengers and an 846 Sqdn Wildcat Mk V are parked at the bow of the TRUMPETER's flight deck after supporting the 22 August 1944 attack on the TIRPITZ. The escort carrier NABOB steams ahead, down by the stern after being torpedoed by the submarine U-354. The NABOB reached Scapa Flow two days later; however, she saw no further wartime service.

Deck handlers aboard the FURIOUS push an 830 Sqdn Barracuda from the lower hangar deck to the deck elevator. A RAF airman supervises the operation from starboard of the aircraft. A Seafire L Mk IIC of either 801 or 880 Sqdn is spotted on the upper hangar deck. The TIRPITZ raids were the last major combat action for the FURIOUS before the carrier was removed from active service in September of 1944.

A Barracuda – believed to be from 812 Sqdn – prepares to launch from the light fleet carrier VENERABLE in April of 1945. A catapult cradle was used in this test with the aircraft. The carrier was training in British home waters prior to deployment in the Pacific. The white dinghy release cable ran from the aft canopy end to the port aft fuselage. The upper wing ASV (Air-Surface Vessel) radar antennas were mounted inboard of the outer wing locking plungers.

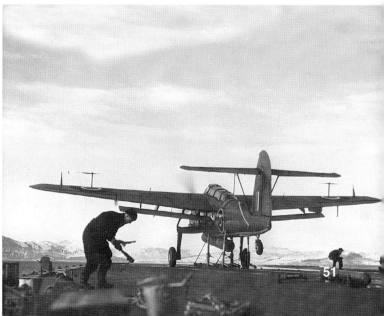

The Far East

The RN carrier strength in early 1942 was limited to HMS HERMES, INDOMITABLE, and FORMIDABLE. The fall of Singapore to the Japanese on 15 February forced the British to move their main Far East base to Ceylon (now Sri Lanka). The mix of Swordfish, Albacore, Sea Hurricane, Fulmar, and Wildcat aircraft was likely to fare badly against the Japanese Mitsubishi **A6M Zero** fighters (Allied codename **'Zeke'**), while the inexperienced FAA crews were faced by combat veterans.

In late March, Japanese Vice Admiral Chuichi Nagumo led the First Carrier Striking Force into the Indian Ocean. Admiral Sir James Somerville, commanding the British Eastern Fleet, divided his force into tactical units, but no direct contact was made with the Japanese – perhaps thankfully, given the enemy's vast superiority in carrier, battleship and aircraft numbers.

On 5 April, Nagumo launched an air attack upon Colombo, Ceylon's capital. Little shipping was on hand, but the Zeros enjoyed a 2:1 'kill'/loss ratio against the Hurricane defenders, as well as wiping out an entire flight of transiting Swordfish. Four days later, a second Japanese force returning from Ceylon after failing to hit the HERMES there caught the carrier southeast of the island. More than 40 bomb hits sent the veteran carrier to the bottom along with her escorting destroyer.

A further RN withdrawal to bases in East Africa and northwest India was deemed wise during the few more weeks Nagumo's force dominated the region. The Japanese eventually retired eastwards for action against the US Navy and never returned in similar strength. The possibility of future Japanese naval ventures in the Indian Ocean and on to Africa had to be considered. The Vichy French-held island of Madagascar was a prime target for occupation, especially since it lay astride the main convoy routes up to Egypt. Action to place it under Allied control began on 5 May. Over 100 aircraft carried by the INDOMITABLE and the ILLUSTRIOUS provided air cover. They also bombed Diego Suarez harbor and its main airfield. The MS.406s and **Potez 63**s encountered by the Wildcats were easily shot down, while the Swordfish and Albacores sank an armed merchant cruiser and two submarines.

RN/USN Co-Operation

By late 1942, the US Navy carrier presence in the Pacific was still seriously eroded, with the four vessels sunk still to be materially replaced by the new ESSEX class carriers. The services of a British fleet carrier were sought and agreed to by the dispatch of the VICTORIOUS. Transit via Hawaii, where the FAA crews provided support for the island's defenses, finally terminated at New Caledonia. On arrival, the VICTORIOUS became part of Task Force 14 (TF 14). The plan of operation was that the **USS SARATOGA** (CV-3) would operate its Douglas **SBD Dauntless** dive-bombers and TBF Avengers in a 'strike' role, while the FAA crews provided fighter cover. The invasion of New Georgia on 21 June 1943 was the force's combat baptism, as well as its sole activity. Along with Guadalcanal-based aircraft, TF 14 supported the landings and guarded against aerial counter-attacks from Rabaul. On 31 July, the VICTORIOUS sailed for home waters. She would return to the Pacific as part of a RN force operating alongside the US Navy, but not before spirited opposition in some military quarters had been raised and defeated.

Royal Navy carrier operations in the Far East were virtually non-existent between late 1942 and January of 1944. During that period, several Fleet carriers operated on their own, while the first CVE for this theater (HMS BATTLER) did not appear until October of 1943. The continued absence of the Imperial Japanese Navy was marginally balanced by a number of German U-boats, whose forays against Allied convoys in the Indian Ocean merited some form of air cover. HMS ILLUSTRIOUS did appear, accompanied by three battleships, in January of 1944. This was in response to reports of several capital ships based at Singapore. In fact, any Japanese vessels located there were simply availing themselves of sound port facilities, having been forced out of their normal Pacific base at Truk, and had no hostile intention towards westward-located targets.

(Left) Two Fulmar Mk Is are spotted on the aft flight deck of the ILLUSTRIOUS during the spring of 1942. Aircraft from this carrier and the INDOMITABLE supported the Allied occupation of Vichy French-held Diego Suarez, Madagascar in May. The Fulmar's wing folding system reduced its wingspan from 46 feet 4.5 inches (14.1 M) to 17 feet 10 inches (5.4 M). The fighters display considerable paint wear from prolonged operations at sea.

(Below) A 703 Sqdn Vought Kingfisher Mk I (OS2U-3; FN709) is secured for raising onto the Armed Merchant Cruiser (AMC) CILICIA in the Indian Ocean during 1943. The aircraft taxied onto a sled towed by the AMC, then was captured by the net placed atop the sled before it was hoisted aboard the ship. The Kingfisher retained European markings although attached to the South East Asia Command (SEAC), whose national markings deleted red to prevent confusion with Japan's red 'Rising Sun' insignia.

The USS SARATOGA, on reverse detachment to the Royal Navy, linked up with the ILLUSTRIOUS in March for a sortie against Japanese cruisers reported off the Cocos Islands. Nothing developed from this operation, but the return to Trincomalee Naval Base on Ceylon saw the vessels and crews preparing for an attack upon Sabang Island, north of Sumatra. The 19 April assault saw Barracudas and USN aircraft striking at shipping and port facilities while covered by Chance Vought **F4U Corsair**s and Hellcats.

Fuel-storage facilities on Java were assaulted next, but Avengers replaced the Barracudas, and the raid was a comparative failure. The SARATOGA then sailed eastward to the United States for a refit.

East Indies Fleet

The East Indies Fleet was properly assembled in May of 1944, with the escort carriers **HMS ATHELING, AMEER, BEGUM,** and **SHAH**. These ships joined the BATTLER in convoy-escort duties. The overall aircraft complement of 150 was supported by five Royal Naval Air Stations (RNAS) on Ceylon. In July, HMS VICTORIOUS and INDOMITABLE also arrived, bringing a further 100 carrier-based aircraft to the theatre. Sabang was again attacked on 25 July, but this time the fleet carriers' contribution was largely in the form of Corsair fighters covering the three bombarding battleships. The Corsairs downed four Japanese aircraft as the fleet withdrew. Barracudas from both fleet carriers damaged facilities on Sumatra in August, but limited intelligence information led to generally poor results. On 17 October – timed to coincide with the US invasion of the Philippines – the VICTORIOUS and the INDOMITABLE mounted a 'diversion' raid against the Nicobar Islands, northwest of Sumatra. One battleship and four cruisers also bombarded the islands. Hellcats 'spotted' for the guns, Barracudas bombed, and the Corsairs strafed. Two days later, a second assault resulted in seven Nakajima **Ki-43** fighters (Allied codename 'Oscar') being downed for three FAA fighters lost. The Grumman Avenger strength exceeded that of the Barracuda, while the ILLUSTRIOUS – back from a refit in South Africa – and the INDEFATIGABLE were on

the scene. The total 1st Aircraft Carrier Force (ACF) aircraft complement exceeded 230 machines. The 1st ACF was reassigned to the British Pacific Fleet (BPF), commanded by Admiral Sir Bruce Fraser, in November, although the force's formal transfer was delayed until January of 1945.

On 20 December, Rear Admiral Sir Philip Vian (Flag Officer of the Carrier Force) sent his aircraft to attack Pangkalan Brandan, a key oil refinery on Sumatra. Thick clouds over the primary target forced the aircraft from the INDOMITABLE (Vian's flagship) and the ILLUSTRIOUS to attack two adjacent oil ports and two airfields, which caused little damage.

The oil refineries at Pangkalan Brandan and Palembang on Sumatra were reported to supply more than half of Japan's aviation fuel supplies. On 4 January 1945, 63 Avengers from the ILLUSTRIOUS, VICTORIOUS, and INDOMITABLE attacked Pangkalan and inflicted severe damage despite heavy Japanese AA fire. The INDEFATIGABLE and the other three fleet carriers launched an attack on the Pladjoe refinery in Palembang on 24 January. The long overland flight to the target and low priority given to fighter sweeps ahead of the bombers gave the Japanese fighters time to assemble in numbers. The Avengers were attacked by Nakajima **Ki-44** fighters (Allied codename **'Tojo'**), while calls for the supporting Fairey **Firefly** two-seat fighters to destroy the barrage balloon sites went unheeded. The resultant diving attack approach through the 'mesh' of balloon cables caused major concern; fortunately, no aircraft struck the cables during the mission. Additionally, the re-assembly point was unfortunately approached over a solid AA defense zone. Only one Avenger was lost to Japanese fighters during this attack, in which 30 percent of Pladjoe's facilities were destroyed. Suitable lessons were absorbed from this raid – defense-suppression, AA-free reassembly points, and proper intercom discipline – in time for the attack against the Soengei Serong refinery complex on 29 January.

The raid on Soengei Serong inflicted greater damage on the Japanese-held oil facilities than the strike on Pladjoe five days before. Two of the Avengers and their crews were lost to barrage balloon cables. Japanese

A US Navy F6F Hellcat lifts off from the VICTORIOUS during joint operations with the USS SARATOGA (CV-3) in the Solomon Islands between May and July of 1943. White wind direction angle lines were painted on the foredeck to aid pilots. The two gun turrets mounted on the starboard side each held two 4.5 inch (11.4 CM) anti-aircraft guns. The ILLUSTRIOUS class carriers each mounted 16 4.5 inch weapons in eight twin-gun turrets mounted around the corners of the flight deck. The VICTORIOUS was relieved on station by the USS ESSEX (CV-9) in August of 1943.

This Swordfish Mk II (KL/LS348) was flown by No 756 Sqdn at Katakurunda, Ceylon (now Sri Lanka) between March of 1944 and February of 1945. The Squadron performed deck landing and refresher flight training for British Eastern Fleet aircrews, using the Swordfish and other aircraft. The fin flash was one-third white and two-thirds blue, rather than the usual half white and half blue flashes used in SEAC.

fighters damaged several Avengers, yet the British aircraft were able to return to their carriers. One Avenger crew turned into a pair of 'Tojos' attacking another aircraft and shot one down! The Avenger of Lt. Halliday (No 854 Sqdn, INDOMITABLE) was hit and caught fire over the target, but he kept the aircraft aloft long enough to reach the sea and ditch beside a British destroyer.

Several Mitsubishi **Ki-21** bombers (Allied codename **'Sally'**) appeared over the British task force while the carriers recovered their aircraft from an aborted airstrike later on 29 January. The scale of AA weaponry on the carriers was nothing compared to their US Navy cousins, but the gunners put up a spirited resistance. Nevertheless it fell to the Seafires forming the Combat Air Patrol (CAP) to 'splash' all seven attackers. Although 16 FAA aircraft were lost to enemy action and 25 others written off or ditched during the assaults, the cost in lost oil production to the Japanese was considerable. Soengei Serong was immobilized for three months and Pladjoe was knocked out for one month. Production never exceeded 50 percent of capacity when it was resumed.

This 1830 Sqdn Corsair Mk II (6C) is parked aboard the ILLUSTRI-OUS following an attack on Port Blair in the Andaman Islands on 21 June 1944. Japanese anti-aircraft fire hit the starboard horizontal stabilizer. Sub-Lt J. Baker of the Royal Canadian Naval Volunteer Reserve was able to bring his Corsair back safely to his ship. The fuselage roundel was retouched to reduce its size.

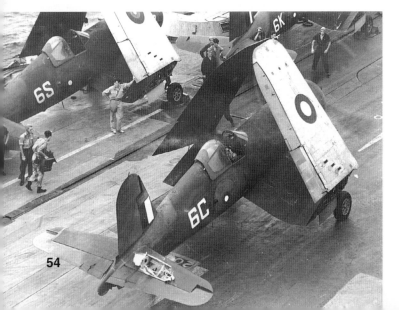

Crewmen gather on the stern of HMS ILLUSTRIOUS to see the USS SARATOGA and her escorts steam away following joint operations in the Indian Ocean in the spring of 1944. Corsair Mk IIs of 1830 and 1833 Sqdns are parked on the flight deck. White and blue SEAC roundels and fin flashes were painted on FAA aircraft operating in the Indian Ocean area from mid-1942. Aircraft from the ILLUSTRI-OUS and the SARATOGA attacked Japanese installations on western Sumatra and Java in the Netherlands East Indies (now Indonesia) in April of 1944.

East Indies Fleet Operations

At the beginning of 1945, the Imperial Japanese Army was being pushed inexorably out of Burma. At sea, the East Indies Fleet (EIF) was now an entirely CVE-equipped entity; all the fleet carriers had departed for the Pacific. The EIF's mission was to support the southward advance of the British 14th Army through Burma and to restrict the movements of the Singapore-based Japanese Cruiser Division. The fighters embarked on the **EMPRESS** and the SHAH were re-assigned to act as a 'pool' for the British Pacific Fleet (BPF).

The first army-support operation was at Ramree Island, Burma (now Myanmar) on 21 January 1945. EIF aircraft flew CAPs and strafed Japanese positions as the Royal Marines stormed ashore. Photo-reconnaissance missions, particularly over the Kra Isthmus and northern Sumatra, were primarily flown during February and March. By April, **HMS EMPEROR, KHEDIVE, HUNTER,** and **STALKER** were 'on station,' bringing the 21st Aircraft Carrier Sqdn (ACS) up to six vessels.

By then, the 14th Army was at the gates of the key port of Rangoon (now Yangon). Four carriers embarked over 100 Seafires and Hellcats for CAPs over the invasion zone, as well as supporting bombing and strafing missions by the Far East Air Force (FEAF). Meanwhile, the SHAH and the EMPRESS steamed off the Andaman and Nicobar Islands, ready to challenge Japanese attempts to reinforce Rangoon. The city fell in swift order on 5 May and the 21st ACS turned its attention to attacking targets further down the Malayan Peninsula. Aircraft aboard the SHAH and the EMPRESS acted as spotters for the guns of the 3rd Battle Sqdn (3BS), when its warships joined in the assault.

In mid-May, the Japanese heavy cruiser HAGURO and other warships attempted to evacuate the Japanese garrison in the Andaman Islands. The cruiser's presence was detected by a British submarine, which resulted in the 3BS and four carriers pursuing the HAGURO. Avengers from the SHAH intercepted the Japanese cruiser on 15 May; however, the airmen scored no hits. Gunfire and torpedoes from five 24th Destroyer Flotilla vessels sank the HAGURO in the Malacca Straits early the next day.

The EIF launched four additional operations prior to V-J (Victory over Japan) Day (2 September 1945). These operations included attacks on airfields, rail and road systems in Malaya and Sumatra, and covering British mine laying off southern Thailand. The fifth operation planned

A DLCO watches an Avenger (5Q) successfully engage an arrestor cable aboard the ILLUSTRIOUS on 17 May 1944. The aircraft had returned from a strike against Japanese-held harbor and oil storage facilities at Soerbaya, Java. Little damage was inflicted on the facilities by aircraft from the ILLUSTRIOUS and the USS SARATOGA. US Army Air Forces B-24 Liberators bombed Soerbaya that evening from bases in the southwest Pacific. This raid caused considerable damage to the harbor and oil facilities.

A Barracuda is 'struck down' (lowered) into the hangar deck of the ILLUSTRIOUS following the raid on Port Blair on 21 June 1944. The flaps and a portion of the wing trailing edge folded over the wing upper surfaces before the outer wings are folded back. Three other Barracudas are spotted on the forward flight deck, along with Corsairs from 1830 Sqdn (6 series codes) and 1833 Sqdn (7 series codes). Deck handlers aft of the elevator await further Corsairs being recovered from the attack.

against Penang was cancelled on 11 August.

The British re-occupation force sailed towards Malaya on 13 September. It was appropriate that the six carriers selected out of the 13 'on station' should be those bearing the strain of action over the past two years or more – HMS AMEER, EMPRESS, EMPEROR, KHEDIVE, SHAH, and STALKER.

Ground crewman tow a 756 Sqdn Barracuda Mk II (KB) past an open-air hangar at Katakurunda, Ceylon in 1944. The bomber was being moved to a dispersal point at the base. No 756 Sqdn was formed in October of 1943 as an operational training unit for FAA units in the South East Asia Command (SEAC) area. Inside the hangar is an Avenger with its wings folded.

An Avenger is brought up from the hangar deck of the ILLUSTRIOUS before a mission against oil installations in Sumatra in December of 1944. Another Avenger is spotted on the bow, while six Corsairs are parked elsewhere on the forward flight deck area. Aircraft from the ILLUSTRIOUS and the INDOMITABLE were launched against the refinery at Pangkalan Brandan, Sumatra on 20 December; however, the strike force hit the port of Belawan Deli due to low cloud cover over the primary target. The cruiser ARGONAUT steams off the ILLUSTRIOUS' port bow. (US Army)

A Fairey Firefly FR.1 launches from the INDEFATIGABLE for a strike against Japanese oil refineries in Palembang, Sumatra on 29 January 1945. The aircraft is believed to be from 1770 Sqdn. The Firefly's four wing-mounted 20MM cannon were augmented by eight three inch (7.62 CM) Rocket Projectiles (R/Ps) under the wings. The two-seat fighter-reconnaissance aircraft was fitted with split flaps on the wing trailing edges.

Deck crewmen fold the wings of a Firefly (K) recovered by the INDEFATIGABLE after the Palembang raid. This aircraft was fitted with 90 imperial gallon (108.1 US gallon/409.1 L) external fuel tanks under the wings, instead of rockets. The undersurface SEAC roundels were smaller in size than the upper surface insignia.

A deck crewman aboard the escort carrier HUNTER checks with the pilot of an 807 Sqdn Seafire L Mk III (D-5L). The fighter stood on its nose while taxing down the flight deck, damaging a propeller blade. The Seafire was camouflaged in Extra Dark Sea Grey (FS36118) and Dark Slate Grey (FS34096) on the upper surfaces and Sky (FS34504) on the undersurfaces. The propeller spinner, fuselage code, and the large wing and tail identification bands were white. White trim was applied around the apertures to the four wing-mounted .303 caliber (7.7MM) machine guns. Two 20MM cannon were fitted to the inboard wing surfaces.

The DLCO directs a Hellcat Mk II (F6F-5) to the catapult of an escort carrier in the Indian Ocean during the spring of 1945. Two deck hands have pulled the chocks from the wheels. A large heraldic shield is painted on the engine cowling, which has a white band on the front. The Hellcat was believed to be assigned to 808 Sqdn aboard the KHEDIVE. This carrier's aircraft supported the liberation of Rangoon, Burma (now Yangon, Myanmar) on 3 May. The French battleship RICHELIEU cruises off the KHEDIVE's port side.

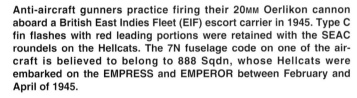

Anti-aircraft gunners practice firing their 20MM Oerlikon cannon aboard a British East Indies Fleet (EIF) escort carrier in 1945. Type C fin flashes with red leading portions were retained with the SEAC roundels on the Hellcats. The 7N fuselage code on one of the aircraft is believed to belong to 888 Sqdn, whose Hellcats were embarked on the EMPRESS and EMPEROR between February and April of 1945.

A Corsair Mk IV (Goodyear-built FG-1D; X/KD747) taxis forward on the escort carrier ARBITER after disengaging its arrestor hook on recovery. The US-built ship arrived in the Far East during the winter of 1944-45, but did not see action. White paint was daubed on the red portion of the fuselage Type C1 roundel. The Corsair is painted overall Glossy Sea Blue (FS15042) with Type C wing roundels.

A 804 Sqdn Hellcat FR.II (F6F-5P) reconnaissance aircraft (6G/JW723) overshot on landing aboard HMS SHAH in April of 1945. The aircraft struck another Hellcat on the forward flight deck, causing extensive damage. A reconnaissance camera window was placed under the fuselage roundel. Smaller SEAC roundels are painted over the larger Type B wing roundels.

Sub-Lts A.J. Bedding (left) and J.P. West-Taylor (right) confer with an 808 Sqdn colleague on the horizontal stabilizer of a Glossy Sea Blue Hellcat Mk II. On 15 April 1945, Bedding and West-Taylor climbed from the KHEDIVE to intercept two Japanese Ki-43 (Oscar) fighters escorting a Ki-48 (Lily) bomber. Bedding shot down one of the Ki-43s in the ensuing dogfight. The Hellcat's fuselage roundel was modified from a Type C1 to a SEAC design.

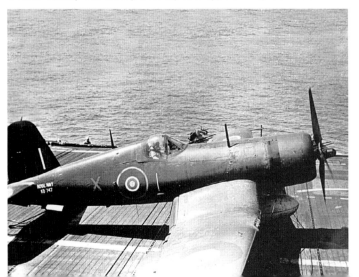

British Pacific Fleet

If the Battle of the Atlantic is regarded as being commenced and sustained primarily by the Royal and Canadian Navies, then the Pacific Theatre belonged even more wholly to the US Navy. When the British Pacific Fleet arrived in 1945, its presence could reasonably be regarded as unnecessary for final victory over Japan. This general view was expressed by Fleet Admiral Ernest J. King, the US Chief of Naval Operations – and not one of Britain's admirers.

All such objections were rejected and the question now was how and where to deploy the BPF. Fleet Admiral Chester W. Nimitz, Commander-in-Chief of the US Pacific Fleet (CINCPAC), regarded the BPF – designated Task Force 57 (TF 57) by the US Navy – as capable of operating independently. One obstacle to this independent operation was the Royal Navy's fleet train, the supply and replenishment ships. The train's mix of vessel-types did not measure up to the custom-built US Navy equivalent.

TF 57 – which included the fleet carriers INDOMITABLE, VICTORIOUS, ILLUSTRIOUS, and INDEFATIGABLE – was assigned to Admiral Raymond A. Spruance's Fifth Fleet. The carriers, two battleships, and four cruisers with destroyer escort sailed from Australia to Manus in the Admiralty Islands. The British warships replenished from their fleet train in the Admiralties before steaming up to Ulithi Atoll in the Caroline Islands. TF 57 then proceeded from Ulithi to their 'station' off the Sakishima Gunto Islands between Formosa (Taiwan) and Okinawa. The Sakishima Gunto Islands were a possible staging point for Japanese reinforcements (particularly aircraft) for the defenders on Okinawa.

The 200 FAA aircraft on hand could attack the Japanese using a mix of heavy machine-guns, cannon, rockets, and bombs. The TF 57 battle plan consisted of operational 'serials' (periods of operations), each lasting two days, followed by two days Replenishment at Sea (RAS). The latter activity was occasionally extended when bad weather arose. On 26 March, a formation of 74 Avengers and Fireflies, escorted by 75 fighters, hit the Sakishima Gunto Islands' airfields. The British force particularly emphasized cratering the runways to make them unusable to the Japanese. Despite the British airmen's efforts, the coral surface rendered itself easy to repair while Japanese AA (anti-aircraft) defenses downed several aircraft.

Combat Air Patrols (CAPs) were a valuable feature of operations, as was proven beginning on 1 April. 'April Fools Day' contained a non-humorous surprise and a small taste of what the Americans were suffering off Okinawa. The ships' radar-operators spotted 'bogeys' (unidentified, believed to be enemy aircraft) approaching from the west. Elements of the CAP, backed by fighters diverted from the island

assaults, were vectored towards the inbound aircraft. The Japanese aircraft flew at greatly different heights from Formosa to TF 57's position, which made the task of mass interception difficult. Several attackers were shot down, but nothing could have warned the FAA pilots of the impending *kamikaze* (Divine Wind; suicide) assaults. The INDEFATIGABLE took a direct strike from an A6M Zero. Its 551.1 pound (250 KG) bomb dented the armored deck and started a small hangar fire. A second 'Zeke' closed in on the VICTORIOUS, but a prompt turn to starboard resulted in the fighter catching the port edge of the deck and cartwheeling into the sea.

For months, the carrier crews had suffered the extreme discomfort of working within what were steel 'sweat-boxes'. Over the ensuing weeks and months, all those who survived the *kamikaze* attacks must have blessed the planning leading to the provision of armored decks. In contrast to the US Navy carriers, whose wooden decks could not sustain major strikes, no BPF carrier was sunk or put out of action for more than a matter of hours. An anonymous US naval officer sailing on the INDEFATIGABLE summed up the situation by saying that a *kamikaze* strike on a US carrier often resulted in months spent in a repair-yard; with a BPF carrier, the crew usually swept the pieces off the deck with brooms. This technical advantage did not make matters any easier for the deck-handlers or other personnel similarly exposed. Additionally, the weight of defensive firepower on the RN carriers was nothing like the concentrations seen on the large ESSEX class carriers.

When the latest 'serial' began on 11 April, the focus of BPF attention was switched to northern Formosa. The airfields located there were regarded as the departure point for the *kamikaze* aircraft attacking both Okinawa and the BPF. These locations were given particular treatment, although bad weather on the first day forced a diversion to Kiirun harbor. On 12 April, two Fireflies of 1770 Sqdn were escorting a PBY 'Dumbo' (Air-Sea Rescue) mission when five Mitsubishi Ki-51 light bombers (Allied codename **'Sonia'**) flew towards Okinawa. The Fireflies intercepted the 'Sonias,' shooting down four of the five Japanese aircraft.

The BPF headed for Leyte in the Philippines towards the end of April for a spell of rest and relief before resuming its normal 'station' southeast of the Sakishima Gunto Islands in early May. HMS FORMIDABLE had replaced the ILLUSTRIOUS and her crew had a horrifying introduction to the Pacific War late in the morning of 4 May. The carriers were without the battleships **KING GEORGE V** and **HOWE**, which were shelling Hirara airfield on Miyako Island in the Sakishima Guntos early that afternoon. Their temporary absence left the carriers dependent upon their own AA weaponry. A 'Zeke' burst through the gunfire to drop a bomb on the center of the FORMIDABLE's flight deck before crashing into the aircraft spotted on the forward deck area. Eight deck-handlers were killed and 47 were wounded, while damage was inflicted on the deck and engine room. Better fortune attended the INDOMITABLE a few minutes

Deck crewmen fold the wings of a recovered 1770 Sqdn Firefly FR.I aboard the INDEFATIGABLE during the early spring of 1945. Retention bars were swung out from the fuselage sides. These bars engaged fittings placed immediately aft of the wing roundels to secure the folded wings in place. The Firefly FR.I's manual wing folding system required a large number of personnel to operate it. Two more Fireflies are positioned further ahead.

This Seafire LF Mk III (H-6Y) of 894 Sqdn makes a hard landing aboard the INDEFATIGABLE during early British Pacific Fleet (BPF) operations in 1945. The nose-up landing sheared off the propeller blades and sprung an engine cowling panel. The wing trailing edges were crumpled from impact with the deck. The Seafire stopped just short of the carrier's crash barrier, which prevented landing aircraft from running into machines parked ahead.

later, when two more *kamikazes* dived almost in line astern. The first was set on fire by AA fire and skidded across the path of the fast-turning carrier before striking the sea. The second 'Zeke' was virtually on top of the after deck when it also faltered and blew up upon impact with the water. The Seafires and Corsairs on CAP above the BPF shot down ten more Japanese aircraft. These 'kills' included six 'Zekes,' two Kugisho **D4Y** attack aircraft (Allied codename **'Judy'**), one Nakajima **B6N** torpedo bomber ('**Jill**'), and one Aichi **D3A** dive-bomber ('**Val**'). The battleships continued their bombardment of Miyako until receiving word of the attacks on the two carriers, then ceased firing to return to the carrier force.

On 9 May, three out of four close-packed incidents involved the VICTORIOUS. First, quick action by the carrier's steersman (US=helmsman) sufficiently threw the *kamikaze* pilot's aim for his aircraft to barely clip the starboard bow AA gun mounts, causing a small fire. A second attacker then dived from astern at a shallow angle, hitting the aft flight deck with a glancing blow before sliding over the side. Four Corsairs were damaged beyond repair from this attack. Finally, a third attacker initially headed for the VICTORIOUS, but then altered course for the nearby HOWE. AA fire from the battleships blew the *kamikaze* apart.

A fourth suicide aircraft then attacked the FORMIDABLE. A 'Zeke' hit the aft flight deck, destroying seven aircraft. Burning fuel from this incident then spilled through the ruptured deck and seriously damaged 11 more aircraft in the hangar deck. The one *kamikaze* was responsible for reducing the FORMIDABLE's 36-aircraft compliment by slightly over one-third. Despite this destruction, only one of the ship's crewmen was killed in the attack. (The incident highlighted the more critical logistical situation on RN fleet carriers compared to their US Navy counterparts, whose aircraft complement was approximately 2.5 times higher than the British carriers.)

The low-level approach tactic employed by recent Japanese attacks led to radar-picket vessels being placed further out from the main body of vessels. The carrier escorts also 'closed up' to provide better AA concentrations. Finally, destroyers were situated directly aft of the carriers to cover the *kamikazes*' favored approach angle.

A third 'incident' affecting the FORMIDABLE was self-inflicted. On 18 May, a Corsair in the packed hangar deck accidentally fired its guns into an Avenger, which exploded. The efforts to control the resulting fires were hampered by an inoperative sprinkler system, which was damaged by the attack on 9 May.

Twenty-eight aircraft were 'written off,' although the carrier was declared 'operational' the same evening.

Task Force 57's first operational spell was closed on 25 May, and the force sailed south for the BPF's home base at Sydney, Australia. Operations ICEBERG (Sakishima Gunto) and ICEBERG/OOLONG (Formosa) had involved an average of 200 sorties for each of the 23 days of action. Only 26 aircraft were lost in action, but 72 others were 'written off' in operational crashes, 32 were destroyed by the *kamikazes*, and 28 were lost in the FORMIDABLE hangar fire.

The INDOMITABLE was withdrawn for re-fitting as World War Two drew to a close, while the ILLUSTRIOUS sailed back to Britain. The latter was replaced by the HMS IMPLACABLE, the last of the ILLUSTRIOUS class ships. In mid-June of 1945, the new carrier was soon in action off Truk Island in the Carolines. The IMPLACABLE then joined the other carriers of Task Force 57, which now shared in Anglo-American air attacks along the Japanese coastline. Just over 250 aircraft were on hand – the same figure for the FAA's total strength in 1939. This total illustrated how greatly (if belatedly) the value of air power to naval operations had been appreciated by the Admiralty.

Admiral Spurance's suggestion that TF 57 fall under the US Third Fleet was accepted by the Third Fleet's commander, Admiral William F. Halsey. (The US naval force in the western Pacific was known as the Fifth Fleet under Spurance's command and the Third Fleet under Halsey.) On 16 July, the BPF (redesignated Task Force 37) departed for the Japanese coast. BPF aircraft attacked airfields around Tokyo and shipping in the Sea of Japan, beginning the next day. On 24 July, aircraft from the INDEFATIGABLE and the VICTORIOUS struck the escort carrier **KAIYO**, moored in Shido Wan Bay, near Beppu on Kyushu Island. Bombs and rockets delivered by waves of FAA

Two 1771 Sqdn Firefly FR.Is (N-278 and N-279) fly a patrol mission over the western Pacific during 1945. BPF carrier aircraft adopted blue and white national insignia with blue-trimmed white bars, similar to the US national insignia. The national insignia on the wings was placed only on the upper port and lower starboard wing section to conform with American practice. Fin flashes were deleted and replaced with letter codes for the carriers; here, N stood for the IMPLACABLE.

Avengers, Fireflies, Corsairs, and Seafires disabled the Japanese vessel – the only carrier ever attacked by RN aircraft. Air opposition was scant; however, on 25 July, the FORMIDABLE's Hellcat CAP downed three of four inbound Aichi **B7A1** torpedo-bombers (Allied codename **'Grace'**).

One of the Pacific War's final actions was an anti-shipping 'sweep' south of Tokyo and off northern Honshu Island on 9 August. Lt R. Hampton Gray, a Canadian, led No 1841 Sqdn's Corsairs from the FORMIDABLE on this mission. The fighters attacked and sank the camouflaged escort **AMAKUSA** off Onogawa Wan. Gray hit the ship with his 1000 pound (453.6 KG) bomb despite being hit by AA fire. The Corsair crashed in flames near the AMAKUSA, killing Gray. (In November of 1945, Lt Gray was posthumous-ly awarded the Victoria Cross – the British Commonwealth's highest award for valor.)

By Japan's agreement to surrender on 15 August 1945, only the INDEFATIGABLE was 'on station' off the Japanese coast. The other fleet carriers had withdrawn to Australia due to fuel shortage. A strafing sortie over Tokyo resulted in the loss of an 894 Sqdn Seafire flown by Lt Freddie Hockley. He bailed out safely, only to be summarily executed by beheading the next day. Hockley was the last FAA airman lost in World War Two.

In this final operational period, Task Force 57/37 had destroyed 347 Japanese aircraft and 356,000 tons (322,963.2 MT) of shipping during 2615 sorties. The British lost approximately 100 aircraft, of which half were lost in action and the remainder to accidents.